Scott Foresman - Addison Wesley
MIDDLE SCHOOL MATH

Practice Workbook

Course 1

Scott Foresman - Addison Wesley

Editorial Offices: Menlo Park, California • Glenview, Illinois
Sales Offices: Reading, Massachusetts • Atlanta, Georgia • Glenview, Illinois
Carrollton, Texas • Menlo Park, California

http://www.sf.aw.com

Overview

Practice Masters provide additional exercises for students who have not mastered key skills and concepts covered in the student text. A Practice Master is provided for each regular lesson in the student text. In addition, a Practice Master is also provided for each Section Review and Cumulative Review lesson.

Lesson worksheets provide exercises similar to those in the Practice and Apply section of the student text.

Section Review worksheets review the student text section and include application problems that review previous material.

Cumulative Review worksheets cover important skills from the chapter at hand and from previous chapters. References to the applicable student text lessons are provided.

ISBN 0-201-31247-6

Copyright © Addison Wesley Longman, Inc.

All rights reserved.

Printed in the United States of America

16 17 18 19 20 21-VHG-08 07 06 05 04

Contents

Chapter 1: Statistics - Real World Use of Whole Numbers

Practice	1-1	1
Practice	1-2	2
Practice	1-3	3
Section 1A Review		4
Practice	1-4	5
Practice	1-5	6
Practice	1-6	7
Section 1B Review		8
Practice	1-7	9
Practice	1-8	10
Practice	1-9	11
Section 1C Review		12
Cumulative Review Chapter 1		13

Chapter 2: Connecting Arithmetic to Algebra

Practice	2-1	14
Practice	2-2	15
Practice	2-3	16
Practice	2-4	17
Section 2A Review		18
Practice	2-5	19
Practice	2-6	20
Practice	2-7	21
Practice	2-8	22
Practice	2-9	23
Section 2B Review		24
Practice	2-10	25
Practice	2-11	26
Practice	2-12	27
Practice	2-13	28
Section 2C Review		29
Cumulative Review Chapters 1–2		30

Chapter 3: Decimals

Practice	3-1	31
Practice	3-2	32
Practice	3-3	33
Practice	3-4	34
Section 3A Review		35
Practice	3-5	36
Practice	3-6	37
Practice	3-7	38
Section 3B Review		39
Practice	3-8	40
Practice	3-9	41
Practice	3-10	42
Practice	3-11	43
Practice	3-12	44
Section 3C Review		45
Cumulative Review Chapters 1–3		46

Chapter 4: Measurement

Practice	4-1	47
Practice	4-2	48
Practice	4-3	49
Section 4A Review		50
Practice	4-4	51
Practice	4-5	52
Practice	4-6	53
Section 4B Review		54
Practice	4-7	55
Practice	4-8	56
Practice	4-9	57
Section 4C Review		58
Cumulative Review Chapters 1–4		59

Chapter 5: Patterns and Number Theory

Practice	5-1	60
Practice	5-2	61
Practice	5-3	62
Section 5A Review		63
Practice	5-4	64
Practice	5-5	65
Practice	5-6	66
Practice	5-7	67
Practice	5-8	68
Section 5B Review		69
Cumulative Review Chapters 1–5		70

Chapter 6: Adding and Subtracting Fractions

Practice	6-1	71
Practice	6-2	72
Practice	6-3	73
Section 6A Review		74
Practice	6-4	75
Practice	6-5	76
Practice	6-6	77
Section 6B Review		78
Cumulative Review Chapters 1–6		79

Chapter 7: Multiplying and Dividing Fractions

Practice	7-1	80
Practice	7-2	81
Practice	7-3	82
Section 7A Review		83
Practice	7-4	84
Practice	7-5	85
Practice	7-6	86
Section 7B Review		87
Cumulative Review Chapters 1–7		88

Chapter 8: The Geometry of Polygons

Practice	8-1	89
Practice	8-2	90
Practice	8-3	91
Section 8A Review		92
Practice	8-4	93
Practice	8-5	94
Practice	8-6	95
Practice	8-7	96
Section 8B Review		97
Practice	8-8	98
Practice	8-9	99
Practice	8-10	100
Section 8C Review		101
Cumulative Review Chapters 1–8		102

Chapter 9: Integers and the Coordinate Plane

Practice	9-1	103
Practice	9-2	104
Practice	9-3	105
Practice	9-4	106
Section 9A Review		107
Practice	9-5	108
Practice	9-6	109
Practice	9-7	110
Section 9B Review		111
Cumulative Review Chapters 1–9		112

Chapter 10: Ratio, Proportion, and Percent

Practice	10-1	113
Practice	10-2	114
Practice	10-3	115
Section 10A Review		116
Practice	10-4	117
Practice	10-5	118
Practice	10-6	119
Practice	10-7	120
Section 10B Review		121
Practice	10-8	122
Practice	10-9	123
Practice	10-10	124
Practice	10-11	125
Section 10C Review		126
Cumulative Review Chapters 1–10		127

Chapter 11: Solids and Measurement

Practice	11-1	128
Practice	11-2	129
Practice	11-3	130
Practice	11-4	131
Section 11A Review		132
Practice	11-5	133
Practice	11-6	134
Practice	11-7	135
Section 11B Review		136
Cumulative Review Chapters 1–11		137

Chapter 12: Probability

Practice	12-1	138
Practice	12-2	139
Practice	12-3	140
Section 12A Review		141
Practice	12-4	142
Practice	12-5	143
Practice	12-6	144
Section 12B Review		145
Cumulative Review Chapters 1–12		146

Name _____

Reading Graphs

Use the Disney Park Attendance pictograph to answer Exercises 1–5.

1. Which park had the
fewest visitors?

_____

2. Which park had the
most visitors?

_____

Disney Park Attendance, 1993

Disneyland ❤❤❤❤❤❤❤❤❤❤

EPCOT
at Disneyworld ❤❤❤❤❤❤❤❤❤

Magic Kingdom
at Disneyworld ❤❤❤❤❤❤❤❤❤❤❤

Disney-MGM Studios ❤❤❤❤❤❤❤❤

❤ = 1 million visitors

3. How many visitors did EPCOT have? _____

4. Which park had more visitors, Disneyland or EPCOT? _____

5. What is the total number of visitors to the four parks? _____

Use the Children in U.S. Families graph to answer
Exercises 6–7.

6. What percent of families include exactly 2 children?

_____

7. Of the categories shown, which is the largest?

_____

Children in U.S. Families

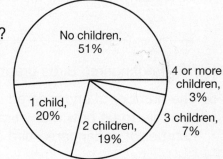

No children,
51%

1 child,
20%

2 children,
19%

4 or more
children,
3%

3 children,
7%

Use the graph of the Five Best-selling Motorcycle Brands to
answer Exercises 8–11.

8. Which brand sold the most motorcycles?

_____

9. Which brand (of the five shown) sold the fewest?

_____

10. About how many Honda motorcycles were sold?

_____

11. Which brand sold more motorcycles, Suzuki or Kawasaki?_____

**The Five Best-selling
Motorcycle Brands, 1993**

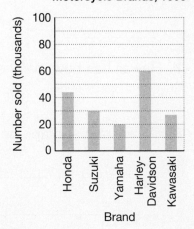

Number sold (thousands)

100
80
60
40
20
0

Honda
Suzuki
Yamaha
Harley-
Davidson
Kawasaki

Brand

1

Name _____

Misleading Graphs

Use the Number of Jobs in the U.S. graph for Exercises 1–4.

1. About how many times taller does the July 1990 bar appear to be than the July 1991 bar?

   _____

Number of Jobs in the U.S., 1990-1992

2. Read the graph. How many jobs were there

   in July 1990? _____

   in July 1991? _____

3. Compare your answers to Exercises 1 and 2. Could the bar graph be misleading? If so, how would you correct the graph?

   _____

   _____

4. How many more jobs were there in July 1990 than in July 1992?

   _____

Use the Endangered Birds graph for Exercises 5–8.

5. The number of endangered bird species in Hawaii appears to be how many times greater than the number of endangered bird species in Texas?

   _____

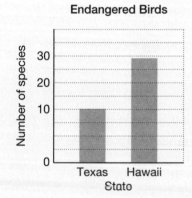

Endangered Birds

6. Texas has how many endangered bird species?

   _____

7. Hawaii has how many endangered bird species?

   _____

8. Could the bar graph be misleading? If so, how would you correct the graph?

   _____

   _____

Name _____

Scatterplots and Trends

For each scatterplot, determine if there is a trend. If there is, describe the pattern of the data.

1. _____

_____

2. _____

_____

Use the scatterplot for Exercises 3–8.

3. Is there a trend? If so, describe the pattern of the data.

_____

_____

4. Name two points that represent people who are the

same age. _____ How old are they?_____

5. Which point represents the youngest person? _____ the oldest person? _____

6. Which point represents the shortest person? _____ the tallest person? _____

7. a. Name two points that represent people who are the same height. _____

b. How tall are they? _____

8. Give the approximate age and height represented by each point.

a. *A*   **b.** *B*   **c.** *C*   **d.** *D*

age _____   age _____   age _____   age _____

height _____   height _____   height _____   height _____

Section 1A Review

Use the bar graph for Exercises 1–3.

1. Which of the armed services had

the most active-duty personnel? _____

the fewest active-duty personnel? _____

2. About how many active-duty personnel were in

the Navy? _____

3. About how many more active-duty personnel
were in the Army than in the Air Force?

_____

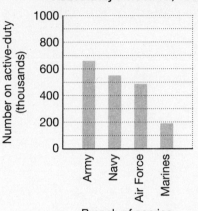

Active-duty Personnel, 1992

Use the line graphs for Exercises 4–6.

4. How much did NASA spend

in 1975? _____

in 1985? _____

5. Describe the change in the data over time.

_____

_____

NASA Spending, 1970-1990

6. How are the two graphs alike? How are they different?

_____

_____

7. Consumer A clock radio sells for $26.00. If a customer
pays $30.00 for the radio, how much change should be
given? Assume there is no tax. *[Previous Course]* _____

8. Last summer Rolando read 17 books. If each book had
236 pages, how many pages did Rolando read all together? _____

Tallies, Frequency Charts, and Line Plots

Make a frequency chart for each set of tally marks in Exercises 1–2.

1. Number of hours of television watched yesterday

Hours	Tally
0				
1							
2					
3								
4				
5			

Frequency Chart

2. Number of pets at home

Pets	Tally
0															
1											
2								
3						
4				
5		

Frequency Chart

3. Make a line plot of the number of books read last month.

Books	Frequency
0	4
1	6
2	3
3	2
4	1

4. The following data set shows the answers people gave when asked how many hours they slept last night: 8, 7, 8, 6, 8, 7, 5, 6, 9, 7, 6, 8, 7, 9, 7

a. Make a frequency chart for the data.   **b.** Make a line plot for the data.

Scales and Bar Graphs

1. Make a bar graph from the data showing the number
of answering machines sold from 1989 to 1993.

Year	Millions of machines
1989	3.7
1990	5.6
1991	8.0
1992	11.1
1993	13.6

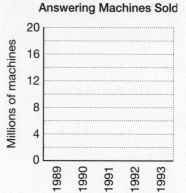

Answering Machines Sold

2. Social Science The data shows the average size of
U.S. households from 1960 to 1990. Make a bar
graph of the data.

Year	Average household size
1960	3.33
1970	3.14
1980	2.76
1990	2.63

Average Household Size

3. What is the range of the data for the average household
size in Exercise 2?

_____

4. Career The data shows the 1990 average weekly
earnings of workers in several industries. Make a
bar graph of the data. Use a broken scale, if
appropriate.

Industry	Earnings
Iron and steel foundries	484.99
Electric and electric equipment	420.65
Machinery, non-electrical	494.34
Hardware, cutlery, hand tools	440.08
Fabricated metal products	447.28

Weekly Earnings

Stem-and-Leaf Diagrams

Use the stem-and-leaf diagram for Exercises 1–4.

stem	leaf
6	7 8 8
7	0 1 2 3 4 9 9
8	1 3 3 3 4 7
9	0 2 5

1. What is the range of the values? _____

2. What value appears most often? _____

3. How many times does the value 79 appear? _____

4. What is the largest number in the data that is less than 90? _____

5. Make a stem-and-leaf diagram of the data showing scores on a history test.

   84, 93, 72, 87, 75, 86, 97, 68, 74, 86, 91, 64, 83, 79, 80, 72, 83, 76, 90, 77

stem	leaf

6. Make a stem-and-leaf diagram of the data showing the number of badges earned by local scouts.

   7, 12, 9, 2, 17, 24, 0, 3, 10, 20, 12, 3, 6, 4, 9, 15

stem	leaf

7. Make a stem-and-leaf diagram of the data showing the number of compact discs owned by some students.

   17, 36, 0, 64, 5, 0, 39, 12, 7, 19, 67, 42, 0, 3, 12, 4, 9, 13, 17, 31, 0

stem	leaf

8. **History** The data shows the number of individuals who served as cabinet members for each of the first 21 Presidents. Make a stem-and-leaf diagram of the data.

			stem	leaf
Washington: 11	J. Adams: 8	Jefferson: 10		
Madison: 16	Monroe: 8	J.Q. Adams: 6		
Jackson: 19	Van Buren: 10	W. Harrison: 6		
Tyler: 21	Polk: 9	Taylor: 7		
Fillmore: 11	Pierce: 7	Buchanan: 14		
Lincoln: 13	A. Johnson: 13	Grant: 23		
Hayes: 10	Garfield: 7	Arthur: 17		

Name _____

Section 1B Review

1. Make a frequency chart and a line plot of the data showing the number of teachers that a set of students have at Monroe Middle School.

   3, 7, 4, 7, 3, 5, 6, 4, 6, 4, 5, 6, 4, 7, 5, 6

   Frequency Chart   **Line Plot**

2. **Geography** Make a bar graph of the data showing the five longest rivers in America. Use a broken scale, if appropriate.

River	Length (mi)
Missouri	2540
Mississippi	2340
Yukon	1980
St. Lawrence	1900
Arkansas	1460

Longest U.S. Rivers

3. Make a stem-and-leaf diagram of the data showing the scores that some students received in a spelling bee.

   23, 36, 17, 21, 42, 19, 30, 22, 61, 20, 19, 24, 18, 26, 21, 19, 20

   stem | leaf

4. Give the approximate weight and price for the package of cereal represented by each point in the scatterplot. *[Lesson 1-3]*

   A: weight _____ price _____

   B: weight _____ price _____

   C: weight _____ price _____

   D: weight _____ price _____

   E: weight _____ price _____

   F: weight _____ price _____

Median and Mode

Find the median and mode(s).

1. median _____

mode(s) _____

| | | | | |
| 23 | 24 | 25 | 26 | 27 |

2. median _____

mode(s) _____

| | | | | | |
| 6 | 7 | 8 | 9 | 10 | 11 | 12 |

3. median _____

mode(s) _____

stem	leaf
1	8 8 9
2	0 3 5 5 7 9
3	1 3 8
4	2 3 5

4. median _____

mode(s) _____

stem	leaf
3	4 6 9
5	0 2 3 7 8
6	1 4 6 7
7	2 3

5. 13, 19, 20, 22, 24, 19, 14, 18, 20, 19, 32, 17, 40, 27, 25, 35, 28.

median _____   mode(s) _____

In Exercises 6–7, make a line plot for each data set, and then find the median and mode(s).

6. 12, 21, 17, 13, 19, 12, 17, 15, 21, 17, 14, 13

median _____   mode(s) _____

12 13 14 15 16 17 18 19 20 21

7. 6, 12, 8, 7, 10, 12, 8, 9, 11, 8, 7, 10, 11

median _____   mode(s) _____

6   7   8   9   10 11 12

8. Find the median and mode(s) for the number of congressional representatives for the southern states:

Alabama: 7   Georgia: 11   Mississippi: 5   Tennessee: 9
Arkansas: 4   Kentucky: 6   North Carolina: 12   Texas: 30
Delaware: 1   Louisiana: 7   Oklahoma: 6   Virginia: 11
Florida: 23   Maryland: 8   South Carolina: 6   West Virginia: 3

median _____   mode(s) _____

The Meaning of Mean

Find the mean of each set of data.

1. mean _____

2. mean _____

3. mean _____

stem	leaf
0	7 7 8
1	0 1 3 8 9 9
2	0 0 1 1 4 6 9
3	0 2

4. mean _____

stem	leaf
3	4 7 8
4	0 1 3 3 7 9
5	1 1 4 6
6	0 1

Find the mean, median, and mode(s) of each data set.

5. 8, 10, 10, 12, 14, 18, 21, 35

mean _____

median _____

mode(s) _____

6. 23, 28, 36, 36, 42, 49, 64, 83, 94

mean _____

median _____

mode(s) _____

7. 41, 18, 63, 24, 37, 72, 84

mean _____

median _____

mode(s) _____

8. 6, 3, 8, 7, 5, 7, 6, 2, 9, 9, 4, 3, 9, 4

mean _____

median _____

mode(s) _____

9. Find the mean, median, and mode(s) of the data showing the number of members of local scout troops.

41, 75, 32, 115, 75, 68, 81, 93, 102, 53, 49, 71

mean _____ median _____ mode(s) _____

10. Find the mean, median, and mode(s) of the data showing the number of points scored by the Hooping Cranes basketball team in their last 12 games.

87, 112, 98, 93, 79, 80, 89, 83, 91, 93, 86, 101

mean _____ median _____ mode(s) _____

The Effects of Outliers

Identify the outlier in each data set.

1. _____

23, 32, 21, 36, 84, 27, 32, 29

2. _____

90, 87, 112, 96, 11, 107, 93, 85

3. _____

stem	leaf
3	6 7 8 8 9
4	0 1 3 3 4 5 7 9 9
5	0 1 1 2
6	9

4. _____

stem	leaf
1	4
3	5 7 8
4	0 2 2 3 5 7 9
5	2

5. _____

stem	leaf
4	8
5	0 1 1 3 5 7 7 9
6	3 4
8	2

6. _____

7. _____

8. a. Find the mean, median, and mode(s) with and without the outliers.

With

mean _____

median _____

mode(s) _____

Without

mean _____

median _____

mode(s) _____

b. Did the outlier(s) affect the mode(s)? _____

the mean? _____

the median? _____

Which did it affect the most? _____

Areas of States (thousands of square miles)	
AK	571
AZ	114
CA	156
CO	104
HI	6
ID	82
MT	145
NV	110
NM	121
OR	96
UT	82
WA	66
WY	97

Name _____

Section 1C Review

Find the mean, median, and mode(s) of each set of data in Exercises 1–3.

1. mean _____

median _____

mode(s) _____

34, 27, 39, 25,
29, 30, 41, 12,
33, 25, 38, 26

2. mean _____

median _____

mode(s) _____

3. mean _____

median _____

mode(s) _____

stem	leaf
2	8 9
3	0 1 3 3 3 4 7 9
4	1 1 2 6 7 7 9
5	0 2 4

4. Use the Wheat Exports graph. *[Lesson 1-2]*

1991 Wheat Exports

a. About how many times taller does the U.S. bar appear to be than the bar for France?

_____

b. Read the graph. What was the dollar value

of French wheat exports? _____

of American wheat exports? _____

c. Could the bar graph be misleading? If so, how would you correct the graph?

_____

_____

5. Make a bar graph of the data showing the number of American households with various pets in 1993.

American Pet Ownership, 1993

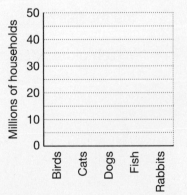

Pet	Millions of Households
Birds	5.4
Cats	29.2
Dogs	34.6
Fish	2.7
Rabbits	2.3

Cumulative Review Chapter 1

Add, subtract, multiply, or divide. *[Previous Course]*

1.   3 8
      + 8 4

2.   8 3 7
       − 1 2 3

3.   3 8 7
      ×   3

4. 6)2322

5. 8)1552

6. 13)2171

Social Science Use the American Grandparents graph to answer each question. *[Lesson 1-8]*

American Grandparents

7. Which age group includes

the most grandparents? _____

the fewest grandparents? _____

8. About how many are in the 45 to 54 age group?

_____

9. Estimate the total number of grandparents shown in the data. _____

The circle graph shows the results of a poll in which people were asked to name the most important factor in sleeping well. Use it to answer each question. *[Lesson 1-1]*

Factors Promoting Good Sleep

10. What percent of those surveyed said exercise was the most important factor?

_____

11. What was the most common response?

_____

Find the mean of each set of data. *[Lesson 1-8]*

12. mean _____

12, 17, 23, 42,
37, 21, 15, 45,
18, 31, 25, 38,
17, 24, 34, 29

13. mean _____

stem	leaf
3	4 7 7 8
4	0 0 2 3 3 4 7 8
5	1 3 3 5 9
6	2 5

14. mean _____

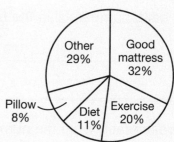

Reading and Writing Large Numbers

Write the number in words.

1. 3784 _____

2. 842,630 _____

3. 7,308,060 _____

Write each state's 1990 population in number-word form.

4. Delaware _____

5. Pennsylvania _____

6. Texas _____

State	1990 Population
Delaware	700,000
Pennsylvania	12,000,000
Texas	18,000,000

Write each number in standard form.

7. 2 million _____   **8.** 63 thousand _____

9. 42 billion _____   **10.** 15 trillion _____

11. Five billion, six hundred fifty thousand, three hundred twenty _____

12. Eight million, seven hundred twenty thousand, two hundred five _____

For each number, fill in the blank. Give your answers in standard form.

13. _____ = 93 billion   **14.** _____ = 2 trillion

15. _____ = 23 million   **16.** _____ = 24 thousand

For each fact, write the number in word form and in number-word form.

17. In 1990, Pepsico had sales of $18,000,000,000.

word form _____

number-word form _____

18. In 1990, the population of New York City was 7,000,000.

word form _____

number-word form _____

Rounding Large Numbers

Round to the given place.

1. 38,721,830, ten-millions

_____

2. 432,483, ten-thousands

_____

3. 1,387,216, tens

_____

4. 83,172,635,810, hundred-millions

_____

5. 392,621, hundred-thousands

_____

6. 471,832,103, millions

_____

7. 217,384,166,982,364, hundred-billions _____

8. 37,852,408,069,843, ten-thousands _____

9. 3,871,664,397,972, hundred-millions _____

10. 6,378,294,183,275, trillions _____

Major league baseball games were attended by 56,603,451 fans in 1990.

11. Write the number of fans in words. _____

_____

12. Round the number of fans to the given place.

a. hundreds _____

b. millions _____

c. ten-thousands _____

d. ten-millions _____

e. thousands _____

f. hundred-thousands _____

13. Thom's kitchen requires 33 feet of wallpaper border. He selects a
design that is available in a package containing a 10-foot length.
Since 33 rounds to 30, he buys 3 packages. Do you agree with his
reasoning? Explain.

_____

Comparing and Ordering Numbers

Order each group of numbers from least to greatest.

1. 3,000; 20,000; 400; 50 _____

2. 38,000; 37,940; 38,010 _____

3. 6,748; 6,847; 6,487; 6,874 _____

4. 3,333; 33,333; 33; 333 _____

5. 78,321; 873,210; 783,210 _____

6. 1,243; 1,342; 1,324; 1,234 _____

7. 99,909; 99,000; 99,900; 90,000 _____

8. 37,630; 37,628; 37,624; 37,700 _____

9. 82,270; 83,100; 82,200; 82,170 _____

10. 48,380; 48,376; 48,408; 48,480 _____

11. 63,821; 63,900; 63,800; 64,000 _____

12. 10 million; 1 billion; 10 thousand _____

13. 1,675; 15 hundred; 2 thousand _____

14. 19 million; 2 million; 30 thousand _____

15. 200 billion; 5 trillion; 990 million _____

16. 18 thousand; 18 million; 180,000 _____

17. In 1990, the Broadway show *Cats* grossed $22,941,820 and *Gypsy* grossed $21,941,875. Compare these numbers using < or >.

_____

18. In 1990, 3,379,000 Americans were employed in food stores, 3,665,000 were employed in transportation, and 3,363,000 were employed in finance. Rank these industries from the fewest employees to the most employees.

_____

Exponents

Write using exponents.

1. $3 \times 3 \times 3 \times 3$ _____

2. 364×364 _____

3. $2 \times 2 \times 2 \times 2 \times 2 \times 2 \times 2$ _____

4. $13 \times 13 \times 13$ _____

5. $8 \times 8 \times 8 \times 7 \times 7$ _____

6. 49 _____

Write in expanded form.

7. 10^4 _____

8. 6^5 _____

9. 3^2 _____

10. 7^3 _____

11. 12^4 _____

12. 5 cubed _____

Write in standard form.

13. 5^4 _____

14. 2^6 _____

15. 11 squared _____

16. 10^7 _____

17. 12^2 _____

18. 6 cubed _____

Compare using $<$, $>$, or $=$.

19. $4^2 \bigcirc 2^4$

20. $4^3 \bigcirc 3^4$

21. $5^8 \bigcirc 5^9$

22. $3^8 \bigcirc 3 \times 8$

23. $2^5 \bigcirc 5^2$

24. $10^3 \bigcirc 10 + 10 + 10$

25. $5^3 \bigcirc 5 \times 5 \times 5$

26. $7^3 \bigcirc 3^7$

27. $10^4 \bigcirc 4 \times 10$

For each number in exponential notation, identify the base, exponent, and power. Use a calculator to write each number in standard form.

28. A typical American kid watches about 18^4 television advertisements between birth and high school graduation.

base _____

exponent _____

power _____

standard form _____

29. The highest point in Kentucky is Black Mountain. Its height is about 2^{12} feet.

base _____

exponent _____

power _____

standard form _____

Name _____

Section 2A Review

Write each number in standard form. Then round that number to the place indicated.

1. 3^4; tens

standard form _____

rounded _____

2. 7^5; thousands

standard form _____

rounded _____

3. 5^4; hundreds

standard form _____

rounded _____

The table lists the 1990 populations of several American cities.

4. Order the populations from least to greatest.

_____

_____

City	Population
Detroit, MI	1,027,974
St. Louis, MO	396,685
Cleveland, OH	505,616
Chattanooga, TN	152,466
Pittsburgh, PA	369,879

5. Round each population to the nearest ten-thousand.

_____

Compare using $<$, $>$, or $=$.

6. 37,990 ◯ 38,000

7. 4^5 ◯ 5^4

8. 630,000 ◯ six thousand, thirty

9. 8,000,000,000 ◯ 8 trillion

10. 7×3 ◯ 7^3

11. 6580 ◯ 64,800

12. The scatterplot shows the number of dogs and cats in several pet stores. *[Lesson 1-3]*

a. Which point represents the store with the most dogs?

_____

How many dogs does this store have? _____

b. Which two points represent stores with the same number of cats?

_____

How many cats does each of these stores have? _____

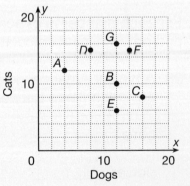

18

Mental Math

Simplify.

1. 60×70 _____   **2.** $162 + 37$ _____   **3.** $142 + 321$ _____

4. $2 \times 21 \times 5$ _____   **5.** 3×81 _____   **6.** $2{,}700 \div 9$ _____

7. $162 + 17 + 38$ _____   **8.** 38×7 _____   **9.** $295 + 85$ _____

10. $28{,}000 \div 700$ _____   **11.** $37 + 42$ _____   **12.** $20 \times 50 \times 37$ _____

13. 100×300 _____   **14.** 62×5 _____   **15.** $875 + 627 + 125$ _____

16. 42×9 _____   **17.** 79×4 _____   **18.** $164 + 135$ _____

19. $8 \times 1{,}200$ _____   **20.** $173 - 98$ _____   **21.** $25 \times 40 \times 17$ _____

22. $38 + 87 + 62$ _____   **23.** $70 \times 3{,}000$ _____   **24.** $600 + 327 + 400$ _____

25. 87×4 _____   **26.** $3{,}800 \div 20$ _____   **27.** $3{,}143 + 222$ _____

28. 300×160 _____   **29.** $20 \times 21 \times 50$ _____   **30.** $387 - 295$ _____

31. 213×2 _____   **32.** $63{,}000 \div 700$ _____   **33.** $750{,}000 \div 2{,}500$ _____

34. $64 + 46$ _____   **35.** $12{,}387 - 4{,}387$ _____   **36.** $38{,}000 \div 190$ _____

37. 52×40 _____   **38.** 39×90 _____   **39.** $5 \times 37 \times 200$ _____

40. $6{,}700 + 1{,}200$ _____   **41.** $8{,}416 - 8{,}116$ _____   **42.** $83{,}725 - 300$ _____

43. $389 + 711$ _____   **44.** $100{,}000 \div 40$ _____   **45.** $320{,}000 \div 400$ _____

46. 310×40 _____   **47.** $56{,}000 \div 800$ _____   **48.** $185 + 32$ _____

49. $90{,}000 \div 300$ _____   **50.** $520{,}000 \div 130$ _____   **51.** $2{,}587 - 198$ _____

52. $64{,}107 - 304$ _____   **53.** $2{,}200 \times 30$ _____   **54.** $63{,}000 \div 90$ _____

55. It takes 300 gallons of water to produce one pound of synthetic rubber. How many gallons of water does it take to produce 8 pounds of synthetic rubber? _____

56. A typical box of personal bank checks contains 200 checks which have been assembled in 8 booklets. How many checks are in each booklet? _____

Estimating Sums and Differences

Estimate.

1. 38,624 + 83,102

2. 47,623 − 12,385

3. 37 + 42 + 43

_____

_____

_____

4. 387 + 410 + 405

5. 824,368 + 217,638

6. 847,167 − 382,208

_____

_____

_____

7. 6375 − 1890

8. 7538 + 2317

9. 163,462 + 3,210

_____

_____

_____

10. 6138 + 5963 + 6023 + 5874 + 6003 _____

11. 69 + 73 + 71 + 68 + 70 + 72 + 67 + 72 _____

12. 894 + 925 + 888 + 907 + 873 + 895 _____

13. 83,762 + 83,984 + 84,731 + 84,201 _____

14. 38,124 + 92,064 + 67,312 + 53,720 _____

15. 1632 + 3129 + 6473 + 3217 _____

16. 867,530 + 9,874 + 128,382 _____

17. 58,128 + 59,370 + 60,028 + 62,310 _____

18. 92,163 + 87,920 + 91,325 + 89,012 _____

19. A world record for dart throwing was set by the Broken Hill Darts Club, who achieved a score of 1,722,249 points in 24 hours. The record score for a women's team is 744,439, achieved by a British team. About how many more points were scored by the Broken Hill Darts Club than by the British team?

_____

20. In 1990, the population of Fresno, CA was 354,202, and the population of New Orleans, LA was 496,938. Estimate the combined population of these two cities.

_____

Estimating Products and Quotients

Estimate.

1. 38 × 47 _____ **2.** 58 × 72 _____ **3.** 867 × 12 _____

4. 163 ÷ 39 _____ **5.** 894 ÷ 293 _____ **6.** 37,183 ÷ 191 _____

7. 79 × 195 _____ **8.** 12,375 ÷ 29 _____ **9.** 5417 ÷ 59 _____

10. 83,921 ÷ 49 _____ **11.** 2414 ÷ 62 _____ **12.** 7398 ÷ 369 _____

13. 8700 ÷ 910 _____ **14.** 3972 ÷ 217 _____ **15.** 732 × 47 _____

16. 55,760 ÷ 692 _____ **17.** 64,900 ÷ 129 _____ **18.** 995 × 24 _____

19. 934 × 193 _____ **20.** 9583 ÷ 163 _____ **21.** 43,972 ÷ 493 _____

22. 72,389 ÷ 8888 _____ **23.** 29 × 817 _____ **24.** 447 ÷ 153 _____

25. 893 ÷ 61 _____ **26.** 95,831 ÷ 398_____ **27.** 143,698 ÷ 119 _____

28. 7862 ÷ 101 _____ **29.** 869 ÷ 27_____ **30.** 621,830 ÷ 7012 _____

31. 4982 × 61 _____ **32.** 350,123 ÷ 698 _____ **33.** 592 × 29 _____

34. 738 × 691 _____ **35.** 1284 × 691 _____

36. 94 × 83 × 41 _____ **37.** 37 × 61 × 59 _____

38. 872 × 6100 _____ **39.** 99 × 41 × 67 _____

40. 6843 × 592 _____ **41.** 13 × 61 × 8127 _____

42. 8397 × 1975 _____ **43.** 367 × 824 × 7 _____

44. 624 × 832 _____ **45.** 384 × 718 _____

46. Akira Matsushima rode a unicycle 3260 miles across the United States in 44 days. Estimate how far he traveled every day.

_____

47. There are 60 minutes in an hour, 24 hours in a day, and 365 days in a year. Estimate the number of minutes in a year.

_____

Order of Operations

Evaluate each expression.

1. $6 \times 3 \div 2$ _____ **2.** $4 + 3 \times 7$ _____ **3.** $12 \div 4 + 2$ _____

4. $36 \div (6 + 3)$ _____ **5.** $8 \times 10 \div 5$ _____ **6.** $50 \div 10 + 15$ _____

7. $13 - 2 - 4$ _____ **8.** $25 - (12 - 10)$ _____ **9.** $(3 + 7^2) \div 4$ _____

10. $(9 - 4)^2$ _____ **11.** 6×2^3 _____ **12.** $(38 \div 19)^5$ _____

13. $8^2 - 5^2$ _____ **14.** $(21 - 15)^2 - 20$ _____ **15.** $600 \div 2 \div 3 \div 5$ _____

16. $125 \div (25 \div 5)$ _____ **17.** $6 \times 5 - 2^2$ _____ **18.** $128 \div 16 - 8 \div 2$ _____

19. $80{,}000 - 6 \times 5{,}000$ _____ **20.** $9000 + 7 \times 300$ _____

21. $21 + 39{,}000 \div 1{,}300$ _____ **22.** $700 - 300 \div 10$ _____

23. $20 \times 7 \div 5 + 11$ _____ **24.** $69{,}000 \div (1700 + 600)$ _____

Insert a pair of parentheses to make each statement true.

25. $3 \times 7 + 4 \times 8 = 264$ **26.** $18 \div 3 + 3 = 3$

27. $8 + 16 \div 4 = 6$ **28.** $500 \div 50 \div 2 \div 5 = 4$

29. $3 \times 2^2 - 1 = 35$ **30.** $48 \div 12 \times 2 = 2$

31. A store has 27 six-packs, 15 twelve-packs, and 34 single cans of soda. Write an expression using the numbers 27, 6, 15, 12, and 34 to show how many cans the store has all together. Do not use parentheses unless they are necessary. Then evaluate your expression to find the number of cans.

_____

32. Find an arithmetic expression equal to 25 that contains the following operations.

a. addition and multiplication _____

b. subtraction and division _____

c. addition and at least one exponent _____

d. division and an exponent _____

Numerical Patterns

Write the number you must add or subtract to get the next number.

1. 3, 10, 17, 24, 31, ... _____ **2.** 88, 87, 86, 85, 84, ... _____

3. 91, 86, 81, 76, 71, ... _____ **4.** 5, 8, 11, 14, 17, ... _____

5. 47, 43, 39, 35, 31, ... _____ **6.** 21, 30, 39, 48, 57, ... _____

7. 225, 240, 255, 270, ... _____ **8.** 144, 132, 120, 108, ... _____

9. 681, 660, 639, 618, ... _____ **10.** 318, 355, 392, 429, ... _____

Find the next three numbers in the pattern.

11. 6, 14, 22, 30, 38, _____ , _____ , _____ , ...

12. 100, 92, 84, 76, 68, _____ , _____ , _____ , ...

13. 20, 30, 35, 45, 50, _____ , _____ , _____ , ...

14. 123, 110, 97, 84, 71, _____ , _____ , _____ , ...

15. 217, 302, 387, 472, _____ , _____ , _____ , ...

16. 5, 11, 23, 47, 95, _____ , _____ , _____ , ...

17. 1, 2, 4, 8, 16, _____ , _____ , _____ , ...

18. 294, 276, 258, 240, _____ , _____ , _____ , ...

19. 20, 24, 30, 38, 48, _____ , _____ , _____ , ...

20. 1, 4, 9, 16, 25, _____ , _____ , _____ , ...

21. 21, 26, 24, 29, 27, _____ , _____ , _____ , ...

22. In 1996, it cost 32¢ to mail a 1-oz letter, 55¢ to mail a 2-oz letter,
78¢ to mail a 3-oz letter, and $1.01 to mail a 4-oz letter. If the
pattern continues, how much did it cost to send a 7-oz letter? _____

23. Science Kris is conducting a science experiment with bacteria.
She begins with 15 organisms. If the number of organisms
triples every day, how many organisms will she have after 4 days? _____

Name _____

Section 2B Review

Simplify using mental math.

1. $8 \times 7 \times 25$ _____   **2.** $127 + 311$ _____   **3.** $60,000 \div 300$ _____

4. $40 \times 5,000$ _____   **5.** $97 + 387$ _____   **6.** $450,000 \div 150$ _____

Estimate.

7. $3,827 + 1,789$ _____   **8.** 364×738 _____   **9.** $58 + 62 + 57 + 61$ ____

10. $5,394 - 1,286$ _____   **11.** $3,842 + 9,169$ _____   **12.** $71,835 \div 5981$ _____

In Exercises 13–16, match the problem and the operation needed to solve it. Each operation is used exactly once.

Sherry's class has 35 students. Carrie's class has 28 students.

13. Sherry's class is split into five equal groups. How _____ many students are in each group?

(A) addition

(B) subtraction

14. How much larger is Sherry's class than Carrie's? _____

(C) multiplication

15. Everyone in Sherry's class shook hands with _____ everyone in Carrie's class. How many handshakes took place?

(D) division

16. Sherry's class and Carrie's class went on a field trip _____ together. How many students went on the trip?

Use the Channel Capacity of U.S. Televisions graph to answer each question. *[Lesson 1-1]*

Channel Capacity of U.S. Televisions, 1993

17. What percent of U.S. televisions had 49 or more channels?

_____

18. Which category included exactly 25% of the televisions?

_____

49 or more channels 45%

37-48 channels 25%

12-36 channels 30%

19. Cedina needs to give a 1293-kilobyte computer file to her friend. Since the capacity of her floppy disk, 1440 kilobytes, rounds to 1000 kilobytes, she is worried that the file might not fit on the disk. Should she be concerned? Explain.

_____

Variables and Expressions

1. Complete the table by evaluating each expression for $x = 2$, 3, and 4.

x	$x + 5$	$17 - x$	$9x$	$\frac{144}{x}$	$x \times 7$	x^2	$5x$
2							
3							
4							

2. Complete the table by evaluating each expression for $x = 3$, 5, and 9.

x	$16 + x$	$x - 3$	$12 \times x$	$90 \div x$	$20x$	$100 - x$	$x \div x$
3							
5							
9							

3. Complete the table by evaluating each expression for $x = 2$, 4, and 7.

x	$x + 43$	$30 - x$	$x \times x$	$x \times 10$	$2x$	$\frac{112}{x}$	x^3
2							
4							
7							

Complete the table.

4. Americans as a whole consume 90 acres of pizza every day.

Number of days	Number of acres of pizza
1	
2	
3	
4	
d	

5. Tennis balls are sold in packages of three balls.

Number of balls	Number of packages
30	
72	
378	
999	
t	

Writing Expressions

Write the phrase as an expression.

1. 12 more than x _____

2. x less than 36 _____

3. one-third of a _____

4. 17 times s _____

5. b multiplied by 5 _____

6. y to the fourth power _____

7. 64 plus k _____

8. u tripled _____

9. p cubed _____

10. 18 minus x _____

11. 4 less than k _____

12. z increased by 12 _____

Write an expression to answer each question.

13. What is the product of 82 and g? _____

14. What is the difference between n and 7? _____

15. What is the quotient of 32 and x? _____

16. What is the sum of h and 7? _____

17. What is 31 less than c? _____

18. What is the fifth power of t? _____

19. What is one-eighth of r? _____

20. Carolyn made t batches of 12 cookies. How many cookies did she make? _____

21. A jar holds n ounces of jam. How many jars are needed for 200 ounces of jam? _____

Write the problem as an expression.

22. **History** Thomas Jefferson was born in 1801. George Washington was born y years earlier. In what year was George Washington born? _____

23. **Science** A spider has 8 legs. How many legs do s spiders have? _____

Using Equations

Is the equation true for the given value of the variable?

1. $x + 5 = 17$, $x = 22$ _____

2. $3 - y = 1$, $y = 2$ _____

3. $4x = 24$, $x = 6$ _____

4. $g - 7 = 11$, $g = 18$ _____

5. $s \div 7 = 3$, $s = 21$ _____

6. $u + 12 = 31$, $u = 20$ _____

7. $h - 13 = 21$, $h = 34$ _____

8. $64 \div n = 16$, $n = 8$ _____

9. $20 \times t = 300$, $t = 160$ _____

10. $18 - c = 10$, $c = 8$ _____

11. $m + 40 = 92$, $m = 50$ _____

12. $x \div 5 = 15$, $x = 75$ _____

13. $3k = 27$, $k = 9$ _____

14. $z - 9 = 61$, $z = 52$ _____

15. $12 + v = 21$, $v = 7$ _____

16. $5w = 20$, $w = 4$ _____

17. $n - 6 = 24$, $n = 18$ _____

18. $k \div 8 = 9$, $k = 56$ _____

19. $m + 12 = 61$, $m = 49$ _____

20. $j + 17 = 86$, $j = 79$ _____

Write an equation for each situation.

21. Jim had 18 CDs. He bought x more. Then he had 21 CDs. _____

22. Rolando baked 4 loaves of bread, each weighing w oz.
The total weight was 80 oz. _____

23. Veronica had m marbles. She gave 5 to Marco. She had
12 marbles left. _____

24. The lunch period at Eisenhower School is normally 35 minutes.
On Thursday, students were given an extra t minutes, so they
had 55 minutes for lunch. _____

25. Stella dealt an entire deck of 52 cards to make h hands.
Each hand had 13 cards. _____

26. Careers The average executive burns an average of
105 calories per hour at work. This is c calories more than
the average secretary, who burns 88 calories per hour. _____

27. Social Studies Each of the 50 United States has s U.S.
Senators. There are 100 U.S. Senators all together. _____

Solving Equations

Find the given value of x that makes the equation true.

1. $\frac{x}{7} = 4$; x = 28, 35, 42, or 49

_____

2. $x - 6 = 13$; x = 18, 19, 20, or 21

_____

3. $5x = 45$; x = 6, 7, 8, or 9

_____

4. $x + 8 = 17$; x = 8, 9, 10, or 11

_____

Find the values for the variable that will provide the given values for the expressions.

5.

u	u + 16
	18
	31
	64
	100

6.

k	6k
	24
	42
	60
	90

Solve the equation.

7. $x + 7 = 30$ _____

8. $m - 10 = 7$ _____

9. $\frac{s}{8} = 13$ _____

10. $11t = 88$ _____

11. $d - 12 = 69$ _____

12. $21 + g = 42$ _____

13. $7u = 35$ _____

14. $n \div 7 = 8$ _____

15. $b - 7 = 24$ _____

Write an equation for each situation and then solve the equation.

16. The top three best-selling albums of all time are Michael Jackson's
Thriller (24 million copies), Fleetwood Mac's *Rumours* (17 million
copies), and Boston's *Boston* (b million copies). The three albums
sold a combined total of 56 million copies. How many million
copies of *Boston* were sold?

_____

17. The main audience section of the Mel Mello Center for the Arts has
9 rows of c chairs. There are 126 chairs all together. How many
chairs are in each row?

_____

Section 2C Review

State whether the quantity should be represented as a variable or a constant.

1. the time it takes you to run 500 yards _____

2. the number of seconds in a week _____

Write the phrase as an expression.

3. x minus 5 _____   **4.** 12 more than p _____

5. the product of 11 and g _____   **6.** 16 divided by d _____

Write an expression to answer each question.

7. Rhonda has u CDs and each of her CDs has 10 songs. What is
the total number of songs in her collection?   _____

8. Max is 48 in. tall. Nell is n in. shorter than Max. How tall is Nell? _____

Is the equation true for the given value of the variable?

9. $x + 17 = 23$, $x = 4$ _____   **10.** $15p = 105$, $p = 7$ _____

11. $42 - k = 19$, $k = 23$ _____   **12.** $\frac{12}{m} = 3$, $m = 36$ _____

Solve.

13. $p - 11 = 38$ _____   **14.** $16z = 48$ _____   **15.** $u + 9 = 64$ _____

16. $7j = 84$ _____   **17.** $\frac{t}{5} = 7$ _____   **18.** $6r = 150$ _____

19. Make a stem-and-leaf diagram of the data showing the estimated
earnings of the ten highest-paid actors and actresses of 1990.
[Lesson 1-6]

Star	$ millions	Star	$ millions	stem	leaf
Sean Connery	28	Eddie Murphy	25		
Tom Cruise	18	Arnold Schwarzenegger	30		
Harrison Ford	13	Sylvester Stallone	24		
Michael J. Fox	22	Meryl Streep	9		
Mel Gibson	9	Bruce Willis	28		

Name _____

Cumulative Review Chapters 1–2

For each plot, determine if there is a trend. If there is, describe the pattern of the data. *[Lesson 1-3]*

1. _____

_____

Price of stereo speakers ($)

2. _____

_____

Height (in.)

Find the median and mode for each data set. *[Lesson 1-7]*

3. 3, 14, 9, 6, 11, 8, 8, 12, 10, 9, 8, 4

median _____ mode(s) _____

4. 37, 42, 38, 41, 38, 43, 39, 44, 40

median _____ mode(s) _____

Write in standard form. *[Lesson 2-4]*

5. 5^3 _____

6. 8^2 _____

7. 11^3 _____

8. 9 squared _____

9. 6^3 _____

10. 2^8 _____

11. 3^5 _____

12. 2 cubed _____

13. Complete the table by evaluating each expression for $x = 2$, 5, and 9. *[Lesson 2-10]*

x	$x + 7$	$50 - x$	$5x$	$x + x$	$180 \div x$	$x \times 7$	x^3
2							
5							
9							

Is the equation true for the given value of the variable? *[Lesson 2-12]*

14. $3x = 15$, $x = 5$ _____

15. $x + 2 = 21$, $x = 23$ _____

16. $\frac{x}{4} = 24$, $x = 104$ _____

17. $37 - x = 25$, $x = 12$ _____

Decimal Notation

What decimal number does each grid represent?

1. _____

2. _____

3. _____

Fill in the grid to represent the decimal.

4. 0.9

5. 0.35

6. 0.72

For Exercises 7–9, write the number as a decimal.

7. six tenths

8. seventeen hundredths

9. two and six hundredths

_____   _____   _____

For Exercises 10–13, write the decimal in word form.

10. 0.63

11. 7.8

_____   _____

12. 0.012

13. 0.09

_____   _____

14. The average American eats three and thirty-six hundredths pounds
of peanut butter each year. Write this number as a decimal. _____

15. A 150-pound person contains 97.5 pounds of oxygen and 0.165 pounds
of sodium. Write both decimal numbers in word form.

_____

Rounding Decimals

Round to the underlined place value.

1. 4<u>2</u>.4   **2.** 7.<u>7</u>961   **3.** 96.<u>0</u>8   **4.** 13.20<u>9</u>3

_____   _____   _____   _____

5. 1.<u>8</u>8   **6.** 3.<u>2</u>92   **7.** 2<u>7</u>.27   **8.** 191.<u>8</u>

_____   _____   _____   _____

9. 796.<u>8</u>4   **10.** <u>8</u>.465   **11.** 59.<u>3</u>05   **12.** 8.0<u>9</u>4

_____   _____   _____   _____

Estimate each object's length to the nearest centimeter and tenth of a centimeter.

13. nearest cm: nearest tenth: **14.** nearest cm: nearest tenth:

_____   _____   _____   _____

15. nearest cm: nearest tenth: **16.** nearest cm: nearest tenth:

_____   _____   _____   _____

17. Measurement One liter is equal to 1.0567 quarts.
Round this value to the nearest hundredth of a quart. _____

18. Colleen's house is made of bricks measuring about 20.955 cm
long, and she guesses that each row in one wall is about
60 bricks long. Estimate the length of the wall.

_____

Name _____

Comparing and Ordering Decimals

For Exercises 1–15, compare using > , < , or =.

1. 0.387 ◯ 0.378

2. 4.8 ◯ 4.83

3. 12.75 ◯ 12.749

4. 8.32 ◯ 8.23

5. 23.65 ◯ 22.66

6. 7.382 ◯ 7.823

7. 32.8 ◯ 32.80

8. 61.23 ◯ 63.21

9. 89.6 ◯ 89.06

10. 5.36 ◯ 6.35

11. 2.75 ◯ 2.750

12. 11.53 ◯ 11.503

13. 38.97 ◯ 39.87

14. 64.381 ◯ 64.38

15. 12.46 ◯ 12.48

Use the graph for Exercises 16–18.

16. Which month has the most rainfall? _____

17. Which month has the least rainfall? _____

18. Which months have the same amount of rainfall?

_____

Monthly Rainfall in London United Kingdom

Order from least to greatest.

19. 21.600, 21.006, 21.060

20. 38.88, 38.888, 38.8

_____

_____

21. 8.23, 8.132, 8.123, 8.213

22. 6.578, 5.687, 5.678, 5.876

_____

_____

23. In 1994, a Greek drachma was worth $0.0041220, an Italian lira was worth $0.0006207, a Mexican peso was worth $0.0002963, and a South Korean won was worth $0.0012447. Order these currencies from the least value to the greatest value.

_____

24. Science An egg laid by a vervain hummingbird weighs 0.0132 oz, and one laid by a Costa hummingbird weighs 0.017 oz. Which egg is smaller?

_____

Scientific Notation

For exercises 1–13, write the number in standard form.

1. 2.87×10^2 **2.** 3.982×10^4 **3.** 5.843×10^5 **4.** 8.95×10^3

_____   _____   _____   _____

5. 5.47×10^6 **6.** 4.638×10^4 **7.** 7.140×10^3 **8.** 1.457×10^5

_____   _____   _____   _____

9. 8.292×10^7 **10.** 1.419×10^9 **11.** 9.47×10^5

_____   _____   _____

12. 4.5185×10^{11} **13.** 6.09577×10^{13}

_____   _____

14. Geography The area of Saudi Arabia is about 7.57×10^5
square miles. Write this number in standard form.   _____

For exercises 15–29, write the number in scientific notation.

15. 38,700   **16.** 16 billion   **17.** 8 million

_____   _____   _____

18. 6,540   **19.** 60,000   **20.** 43,950

_____   _____   _____

21. 85 trillion   **22.** 682,300   **23.** 2,137,000

_____   _____   _____

24. 238,000,000   **25.** 560,000,000   **26.** 341,700,000

_____   _____   _____

27. 4,382,000,000,000   **28.** 5,863,000,000,000   **29.** 493,000,000,000

_____   _____   _____

30. Astronomy The sun is about 149,597,900 km away
from Earth. Write this number in scientific notation.   _____

Name _____

Section 3A Review

Write as a decimal.

1. $\dfrac{27}{100}$

2. $\dfrac{63}{1000}$

3. eight and seven tenths

_____   _____   _____

Measure each object to the nearest centimeter.

4. _____

5. _____

Round to the underlined place value.

6. 3.8<u>7</u>5   **7.** <u>6</u>.241   **8.** 9.3<u>1</u>6   **9.** 2.1<u>4</u>9

_____   _____   _____   _____

10. Health The average person produces enough
saliva in a lifetime to fill a swimming pool, about
1.2×10^6 fl oz. Write this number in standard form.   _____

Write the number in standard form.

11. 3.89×10^4 _____   **12.** 7.13×10^2 _____   **13.** 8.3×10^5 _____

Write the number in scientific notation.

14. 7 billion _____   **15.** 6,510,000 _____

16. Science The line plot shows the duration (in days) of each space
shuttle mission conducted by any nation from 1988–1990. *[Lesson 1-9]*

   a. Find the mean, median, and mode(s) of the data.

     mean _____   median _____   mode(s) _____

   b. Did the outlier affect the mean? _____

17. Lance earns $80 per day at his job. If he worked
200 days last year, how much did he earn? *[Lesson 2-5]*   _____

Name _____

Estimating with Decimals

Estimate each sum, difference, product, or quotient.

1. 3.68 + 1.75

2. 38.73 × 7.9

3. 12.837 − 2.14

4. 63.917 ÷ 7.6

_____   _____   _____   _____

5. 13.6875 + 7.94

6. 18.374 − 8.47

7. 31.27 × 5.837

8. 75.59 ÷ 4.23

_____   _____   _____   _____

9. 81.238 + 61.59

10. 163.94 − 39.4

11. $8.47 × 7.31

12. 15.83 ÷ 3.57

_____   _____   _____   _____

13. 8.743 + 9.14

14. 28.6 − 13.14

15. 8.138 × 7.2

16. 39.61 ÷ 4.83

_____   _____   _____   _____

17. 3.941 + 14.83

18. 68.1 − 15.23

19. 3.6 × 5.12

20. 96.3 ÷ 6.41

_____   _____   _____   _____

21. 1.09 + 3.06

22. $53.82 − $16.24

23. 18.39 × 1.94

24. 56.43 ÷ 13.8

_____   _____   _____   _____

25. 8.3 + 12.741

26. 38.89 − 15.63

27. 21.4 × 5.2

28. 196.4 ÷ 6.9

_____   _____   _____   _____

29. 37.14 + 9.3

30. 103.45 − 23.2

31. 9.74 × 39.1

32. 35.74 ÷ 5.63

_____   _____   _____   _____

33. You go to a garage sale where all books are priced at $0.35.

   a. About how many books could you buy for $10.00? _____

   b. Miguel bought 18 books. About how much did he pay? _____

34. Tonja has 3 dogs which are all about the same size. If the
dogs weigh a total of 83.4 lb, estimate the weight of each dog. _____

35. Fred wants to buy a $15.95 CD and a $9.35 book. He has
$24.00. Does he have enough money for the two items? _____

Adding and Subtracting Decimal Numbers

Simplify.

1. 2.84 + 1.9

2. 3.824 − 1.73

3. 9.876 + 1.349

4. 8.67 − 4.21

_____   _____   _____   _____

5. $3.87 + $12.43

6. 21.874 − 3.69

7. 5.3 + 8.49

8. 24.3 − 7.631

_____   _____   _____   _____

9. 5.87 + 9.321

10. 8.743 − 2.38

11. 5.61 + 21.379

12. 5.3 − 2.1483

_____   _____   _____   _____

13. 9.6413 − 2.14

14. 8.365 + 9.3

15. 12.67 − 10

16. 43 + 5.374

_____   _____   _____   _____

17. 39.74 − 5.678

18. 21.473 + 8.2

19. 193.8 − 21.73

20. $84.67 + $91.49

_____   _____   _____   _____

21. 36.04 + 9.87

22. 56.583 − 39.42

23. $48.43 − $27.62

24. 394.2 + 7.165

_____   _____   _____   _____

25. 2.375 + 6.841 + 9.3894

26. 8.23 + 12.7 + 6.74 + 9.32

_____   _____

27. 7.124 + 8.1 + 9.32 + 7

28. 9.45 + 6.38 + 7.42 + 21.63

_____   _____

29. Three lizards weighing 1.57 oz, 1.438 oz, and 1.6412 oz are in a cage. What is their combined weight? _____

30. Science Jupiter rotates once every 9.925 hr, and Saturn rotates once every 10.673 hr. Saturn's rotation is how much longer than Jupiter's rotation? _____

Name _____

Solving Decimal Equations: Addition and Subtraction

Solve.

1. $h + 3.6 = 8.6$

$h =$ _____

2. $b - 7 = 12.3$

$b =$ _____

3. $9 + t = 12.4$

$t =$ _____

4. $10 - a = 3.4$

$a =$ _____

5. $r + 2.2 = 5.7$

$r =$ _____

6. $n - 6.2 = 11.4$

$n =$ _____

7. $8 + j = 15.34$

$j =$ _____

8. $14.3 - g = 6.3$

$g =$ _____

9. $m + 7.3 = 9.1$

$m =$ _____

10. $d - 10.3 = 1.8$

$d =$ _____

11. $6.3 + f = 10.5$

$f =$ _____

12. $3.9 - c = 3.1$

$c =$ _____

13. $q + \$18.3 = \$20$

$q =$ _____

14. $k - 5.1 = 2.9$

$k =$ _____

15. $3.89 + x = 5.2$

$x =$ _____

16. $18.4 - u = 9.6$

$u =$ _____

17. $e + 2.7 = 10$

$e =$ _____

18. $r - 7.5 = 3.1$

$r =$ _____

19. $5.62 + p = 5.99$

$p =$ _____

20. $8.3 - y = 2.7$

$y =$ _____

Geometry Given the distance around the shape, find the length of the unknown side.

21. Total distance: 31.9 cm

$w =$ _____

10.8 cm   w

8.7 cm

22. Total distance: 62.5 m

$v =$ _____

9.1 m

v

18.1 m

13.4 m

23. Yesterday Stephanie spent $38.72 on new shoes and $23.19 on computer software. When she was finished, she had $31.18. How much money did she have before she went shopping?

_____

24. The owner of a used music store bought a compact disc for $4.70 and sold it for $9.45. Write and solve an equation to find the profit.

_____

Name _____

Section 3B Review

Estimate the length to the nearest tenth of a centimeter.

1. _____

2. _____

Write each number in decimal form.

3. eight and thirty-two hundredths

_____

4. sixty-five thousandths

_____

Simplify.

5. $8.73 - 5.2$ _____

6. $12.3 + 6.84$ _____

7. $21.37 - 6.41$ _____

Find the distance around the shape.

8. _____

9. _____

10. _____

Solve.

11. $c + 3.4 = 7.5$

$c =$ _____

12. $13.2 - p = 9.7$

$p =$ _____

13. $15 + h = 24.3$

$h =$ _____

14. Rick has $100 in his wallet. He wants to buy a clock for $34, a comforter for $44, and a pair of jeans for $24. Since he has estimated the sum as $30 + $40 + $20 = $90, he is confident that he has enough money for his purchases. Do you agree? Explain. *[Lesson 2-6]*

_____

15. Jennifer bought some stock for $24 per share. For the next 6 months, the stock increased in value each month by $3 per share. How much was each share worth 6 months after she bought it? *[Lesson 2-9]*

_____

Multiplying a Whole Number by a Decimal

Insert a decimal point in the answer to make the equation true.

1. 12 × 8.76 = 1 0 5 1 2   **2.** 4.67 × 7 = 3 2 6 9   **3.** 3.375 × 8 = 2 7 0 0 0

4. 7 × 2.831 = 1 9 8 1 7   **5.** 9.26 × 15 = 1 3 8 9 0   **6.** 2.36 × 21 = 4 9 5 6

7. 10 × 4.63 = 4 6 3 0   **8.** 17 × 9.37 = 1 5 9 2 9   **9.** 5.63 × 8 = 4 5 0 4

10. 7.41 × 16 = 1 1 8 5 6   **11.** 1.01 × 7 = 7 0 7   **12.** 3.94 × 4 = 1 5 7 6

Multiply.

13. 2.76 × 10   **14.** 2.76 × 100   **15.** 2.76 × 1000   **16.** 8.137 × 20

_____   _____   _____   _____

17. 61 × 4.731   **18.** 15.167 × 15   **19.** 6 × 26.34   **20.** 18.5 × 3

_____   _____   _____   _____

21. 10 × 18.438   **22.** $3.94 × 5   **23.** 31.2 × 1000   **24.** 4 × 16.81

_____   _____   _____   _____

25. 2 × 18.3876   **26.** 13 × 5.61   **27.** 6.25 × 12   **28.** 4.39 × 10

_____   _____   _____   _____

29. 4.161 × 5   **30.** 8 × $11.72   **31.** 14 × 31.347   **32.** 17.4 × 9

_____   _____   _____   _____

33. 17 × 3.17   **34.** 5.631 × 11   **35.** 1000 × 9.34   **36.** 8 × 3.812

_____   _____   _____   _____

37. A can contains 0.17 kg of tomato paste.
How much tomato paste would be in 8 cans?   _____

38. In a typical day, Cheryl works for 8 hours at the rate
of $7.61 per hour. She also buys lunch for $5.43.
How much does she have at the end of the day?   _____

Multiplying a Decimal by a Decimal

Insert a decimal point in the answer to make the equation true.

1. $3.7 \times 19.8 = 7\ 3\ 2\ 6$

2. $5.7 \times 19.9 = 1\ 1\ 3\ 4\ 3$

3. $2.9 \times 13.82 = 4\ 0\ 0\ 7\ 8$

4. $10.2 \times 9.49 = 9\ 6\ 7\ 9\ 8$

5. $12.14 \times 8 = 9\ 7\ 1\ 2$

6. $16.6 \times 7.1 = 1\ 1\ 7\ 8\ 6$

7. $3.0 \times 5.18 = 1\ 5\ 5\ 4$

8. $10.9 \times 10.611 = 1\ 1\ 5\ 6\ 5\ 9\ 9$

Multiply.

9. 9.031×0.5

10. 0.01×9.1

11. 50.9×0.9

12. 0.6×0.07

_____ _____ _____ _____

13. 0.2×0.278

14. 9.2×0.25

15. 5.6×4.8

16. 0.02×0.3

_____ _____ _____ _____

17. 0.6×0.005

18. 55.5×0.07

19. 0.3×38.8

20. 0.5×2.1

_____ _____ _____ _____

21. 0.01×7.3

22. 52.62×0.8

23. 0.42×0.2

24. 7.07×4.9

_____ _____ _____ _____

25. A health food store sells granola for $1.80 per
pound. How much would 1.3 pounds of granola cost? _____

26. Health Raw broccoli has 0.78 mg of iron per cup.
How much iron is in 2.3 cups of broccoli? _____

Compare using $<$, $>$, or $=$.

27. $6.14 \times 0.25 \bigcirc 61.4 \times 2.5$

28. $0.03 \times 12.4 \bigcirc 0.3 \times 1.24$

29. $5.2 \times 62.9 \bigcirc 0.52 \times 6.29$

30. $4.7 \times 8.17 \bigcirc 4.7 \times 81.7$

31. $7.0 \times 1.72 \bigcirc 0.07 \times 172.0$

32. $8.54 \times 27.0 \bigcirc 85.4 \times 2.7$

33. Consumer If gasoline costs $1.539 per gallon, how much
would you pay for 12.64 gallons? (Round your answer to
the nearest cent.) _____

Dividing by a Whole Number

Insert a decimal point in the answer to make the equation true.

1. 37.164 ÷ 76 = 0 4 8 9   **2.** 110.24 ÷ 32 = 3 4 4 5   **3.** 41.34 ÷ 6 = 6 8 9

4. 320.662 ÷ 67 = 4 7 8 6   **5.** 143.68 ÷ 20 = 7 1 8 4   **6.** 15.9 ÷ 3 = 5 3

7. 6.3 ÷ 7 = 0 9   **8.** 17.505 ÷ 3 = 5 8 3 5   **9.** 6.532 ÷ 4 = 1 6 3 3

Divide.

10. 33.628 ÷ 14   **11.** 111.618 ÷ 39   **12.** 22.8 ÷ 19   **13.** 257.24 ÷ 59

_____   _____   _____   _____

14. 162.5 ÷ 65   **15.** 27.23 ÷ 7   **16.** 16.668 ÷ 3   **17.** 23.94 ÷ 63

_____   _____   _____   _____

18. 190.4 ÷ 28   **19.** 23.58 ÷ 20   **20.** 20.305 ÷ 5   **21.** 0.931 ÷ 19

_____   _____   _____   _____

22. 90.034 ÷ 59   **23.** 385.92 ÷ 48   **24.** 179.8 ÷ 58   **25.** 5.337 ÷ 3

_____   _____   _____   _____

26. 36.11 ÷ 23   **27.** 244.29 ÷ 51   **28.** 150.92 ÷ 49   **29.** 15.98 ÷ 47

_____   _____   _____   _____

30. 503.7 ÷ 69   **31.** 12.6 ÷ 42   **32.** 4.14 ÷ 9   **33.** 113.26 ÷ 14

_____   _____   _____   _____

34. 465.272 ÷ 76   **35.** 469.7 ÷ 61   **36.** 8.6 ÷ 86   **37.** 13.425 ÷ 15

_____   _____   _____   _____

38. Keith paid $24.57 for 9 blank videotapes.
How much did each tape cost?   _____

39. In 1988, a team of 32 divers set a record by pedaling
a tricycle 116.66 miles underwater. Find the mean
distance pedaled by each diver.   _____

Dividing by a Decimal

Insert a decimal point in the answer to make the equation true.

1. $7.4096 \div 1.1 = 6\ 7\ 3\ 6$ **2.** $22.3443 \div 5.49 = 4\ 0\ 7$ **3.** $3.1515 \div 1.5 = 2\ 1\ 0\ 1$

4. $4.8225 \div 2.5 = 1\ 9\ 2\ 9$ **5.** $17.22 \div 4.1 = 4\ 2\ 0$ **6.** $12.576 \div 2.4 = 5\ 2\ 4$

Divide.

7. $11.5213 \div 0.7$ **8.** $5.18 \div 0.7$ **9.** $8.7 \div 4.35$ **10.** $37.014 \div 5.97$

_____   _____   _____   _____

11. $0.3798 \div 0.18$ **12.** $0.65232 \div 13.59$ **13.** $100.859 \div 8.65$ **14.** $0.51272 \div 0.754$

_____   _____   _____   _____

15. $1.8136 \div 0.2$ **16.** $46.2 \div 16.5$ **17.** $3.915 \div 13.05$ **18.** $1.44 \div 1.6$

_____   _____   _____   _____

19. $20.013 \div 2.1$ **20.** $0.65355 \div 0.15$ **21.** $1.265 \div 0.23$ **22.** $19.76 \div 2.6$

_____   _____   _____   _____

23. $2.2242 \div 0.33$ **24.** $46.02 \div 3.9$ **25.** $1.512 \div 0.672$ **26.** $0.061 \div 0.1$

_____   _____   _____   _____

27. $3.86 \div 3.86$ **28.** $7.896 \div 3.29$ **29.** $9.8072 \div 5.33$ **30.** $3.0768 \div 0.8$

_____   _____   _____   _____

31. $0.908 \div 4.54$ **32.** $0.056 \div 1.4$ **33.** $9.57 \div 2.9$ **34.** $0.414 \div 4.6$

_____   _____   _____   _____

35. $92.7 \div 12.36$ **36.** $1.9312 \div 1.136$ **37.** $18.65 \div 2.5$ **38.** $132.16 \div 11.2$

_____   _____   _____   _____

39. Science Jupiter revolves around the Sun once every
11.86 years. How many times does it revolve in 40.324 years? _____

40. Health 4.7 oz of pistachio nuts contain 1.786 mg
of zinc. How much zinc is in 1 oz of pistachios? _____

Name _____

Solving Decimal Equations: Multiplication and Division

Solve.

1. $4n = 1.72$

$n =$ _____

2. $\dfrac{d}{2.5} = 1.263$

$d =$ _____

3. $0.9g = 9.99$

$g =$ _____

4. $1.9v = 9.025$

$v =$ _____

5. $\dfrac{r}{0.8} = 11.279$

$r =$ _____

6. $\dfrac{n}{0.5} = 1.537$

$n =$ _____

7. $1.2k = 7.968$

$k =$ _____

8. $\dfrac{s}{0.85} = 2.4$

$s =$ _____

9. $8.3y = 28.967$

$y =$ _____

10. $\dfrac{a}{5.5} = 6.25$

$a =$ _____

11. $5.9c = 8.555$

$c =$ _____

12. $\dfrac{x}{8.1} = 6.31$

$x =$ _____

13. $8.5t = 77.18$

$t =$ _____

14. $\dfrac{b}{3.5} = 6.5$

$b =$ _____

15. $1.1s = 0.726$

$s =$ _____

16. $\dfrac{w}{13} = 0.12$

$w =$ _____

17. $0.1t = 1.1$

$t =$ _____

18. $\dfrac{m}{6.7} = 1.57$

$m =$ _____

19. $3.59p = 4.308$

$p =$ _____

20. $\dfrac{k}{4.67} = 10.8$

$k =$ _____

21. $0.15n = 1.3575$

$n =$ _____

22. $\dfrac{d}{0.243} = 0.1$

$d =$ _____

23. $0.65p = 0.5395$

$p =$ _____

24. $\dfrac{m}{3.902} = 5$

$m =$ _____

25. $\dfrac{r}{0.35} = 2.76$

$r =$ _____

26. $\dfrac{c}{4.1} = 5.48$

$c =$ _____

27. $\dfrac{u}{6.9} = 10.3$

$u =$ _____

28. $8.77m = 6.139$

$m =$ _____

29. $2.94q = 7.35$

$q =$ _____

30. $5.6t = 58.8$

$t =$ _____

31. $0.8d = 9.816$

$d =$ _____

32. $13.41w = 17.433$

$w =$ _____

For Exercises 33 and 34, set up an equation and solve.

33. Yesterday Helen used one-seventh of the vegetable oil in her kitchen. If she used 2.43 oz, how much did she have originally? _____

34. Consumer In 1994, the Louisiana sales tax on an item was 0.04 times the price of the item. If Tom paid $1.09 in sales tax when he bought a shirt, what was the price of the shirt? _____

Section 3C Review

Simplify.

1. 3 × 0.63

2. 0.016 × 0.02

3. 205.65 ÷ 15

4. 26 × 0.009

_____ _____ _____ _____

5. 16.936 ÷ 73

6. 36 × 0.11

7. 0.05 × 4.9

8. 245.49 ÷ 30

_____ _____ _____ _____

9. 7 × 0.05

10. 0.07 × 0.845

11. 140.6 ÷ 37

12. 27.216 ÷ 17.01

_____ _____ _____ _____

Write the number in standard form.

13. 3.84×10^3

14. 1.789×10^5

15. 6.4432×10^6

_____ _____ _____

16. 6.387×10^9

17. 8.3764×10^4

18. 4.3857×10^{10}

_____ _____ _____

Solve.

19. $4.63a = 12.964$ **20.** $\dfrac{d}{6.21} = 8.9$ **21.** $5w = 15.05$ **22.** $\dfrac{k}{0.81} = 7.39$

$a =$ _____ $d =$ _____ $w =$ _____ $k =$ _____

23. $1.4f = 0.0882$ **24.** $0.9w = 0.5634$ **25.** $10.6g = 1.166$ **26.** $\dfrac{t}{4.61} = 6.7$

$f =$ _____ $w =$ _____ $g =$ _____ $t =$ _____

27. Five bunches of broccoli weigh 0.94 lb, 1.27 lb, 0.83 lb, 1.07 lb, and 0.98 lb. What is the average of these weights? _____

28. **Science** A goat typically lives 4 times as long as a rat. A rat's lifetime lasts *t* years. Write an expression to show how long a goat lives. _____

29. In 1974, the federal minimum wage was $2.00 per hour. Use mental math to determine how much a worker earning minimum wage would be paid for working 38 hours. *[Lesson 2-5]* _____

Name _____

Practice

Cumulative Review Chapters 1–3

Use the 1992 Election Results graph to answer each question. *[Lesson 1-1]*

1. Who had the most votes? _____

2. About how many people voted for Ross Perot?

_____

3. Estimate the total number of votes shown in the data.

_____

1992 Presidential Election Results

(bar graph: Votes (millions) on vertical axis, scale 0 to 50; George Bush ≈ 39, Bill Clinton ≈ 45, Ross Perot ≈ 20)

Round to the given place. *[Lesson 2-2]*

4. 27,341, thousands

5. 3,137,621, hundred-thousands

_____   _____

For Exercises 6–11, compare using <, >, or =. *[Lesson 3-3]*

6. 3.9 ◯ 3.87   **7.** 7.03 ◯ 7.30   **8.** 9.26 ◯ 9.62

9. 3.4 ◯ 4.3   **10.** 8.64 ◯ 8.640   **11.** 12.75 ◯ 12.7499

Estimate each sum, difference, product, or quotient. *[Lesson 3-5]*

12. 12.63 + 4.07   **13.** 3.96 − 1.24   **14.** $9.14 × 7.2   **15.** 26.64 ÷ 8.73

_____   _____   _____   _____

16. $3.84 + $5.62   **17.** 11.49 − 2.36   **18.** 9.1 × 4.873   **19.** 119.6 × 20.4

_____   _____   _____   _____

Solve using inverse operations. *[Lesson 3-12]*

20. $0.6p = 3.12$ **21.** $\dfrac{m}{6.9} = 0.47$ **22.** $6.18v = 3.0282$ **23.** $1.6t = 13.344$

$p =$ _____ $m =$ _____ $v =$ _____ $t =$ _____

24. $\dfrac{w}{1.61} = 4.3$ **25.** $\dfrac{x}{8.7} = 0.25$ **26.** $0.39a = 3.276$ **27.** $\dfrac{a}{1.8} = 5.87$

$w =$ _____ $x =$ _____ $a =$ _____ $a =$ _____

Name _____

Perimeter

Find the perimeter.

1. _____

4 cm
6 cm

2. _____

9 ft 12 ft
15 ft

3. _____

3 m
3 m

4. _____

1.4 mi
0.35 mi

5. _____

4 in.
4 in.
2 in.
5 in.

6. _____

11 km
8 km
3 km 3 km
4 km 4 km

Find the lengths of each unknown side.

7. *a* = _____ *b* = _____

7 cm
b *a*
6 cm   8 cm
11 cm

8. *c* = _____ *d* = _____

12 in.
12 in.   *c*
16 in.
4 in.
d

9. *x* = _____ *y* = _____

7 ft
3 ft
x
8 ft   *y*
4 ft
3 ft
8 ft

10. *p* = _____ *q* = _____

p
6 m   *q*
2 m   3 m
2 m   2 m
8 m

11. *f* = _____ *g* = _____

33 cm
6 cm
f 21 cm
15 cm
g

12. *t* = _____ *u* = _____

4 mi
8 mi
16 mi   *t*
4 mi
8 mi   *u*
17 mi

13. The triangular base of a skyscraper has a perimeter of 89 m. If two of the sides have lengths 30 m and 35 m, what is the length of the third side?

_____

Name _____

Converting in the Metric System

For Exercises 1–10, name an appropriate metric unit of measure.

1. Weight of a calculator _____

2. Height of a woman _____

3. Amount of gasoline in a car _____

4. Distance from Hong Kong to
   Beijing, China _____

5. Weight of a paper clip _____

6. Length of an airplane _____

7. Amount of coffee in a cup _____

8. Weight of a golden retriever _____

9. Width of a playing card _____

10. Amount of glue used to repair a plate _____

Convert.

11. 4 m = _____ cm 12. 39 g = _____ kg 13. 87 cm = _____ m

14. 2.7L = _____ mL 15. 4.3 km = _____ m 16. 14.2 kg = _____ g

17. 538 mL = _____ L 18. 3.7 g = _____ kg 19. 7.4 m = _____ km

20. 21 cm = _____ mm 21. 42 m = _____ km 22. 0.8 km = _____ cm

23. 43 mm = _____ cm 24. 8.26 kg = _____ g 25. 2.3 km = _____ cm

26. **Science** A tornado typically moves about 64,400 meters
    in an hour. Convert this distance to kilometers. _____

27. **Geography** Kazakhstan has about 2,320 km
    of coastline. Convert this distance to millimeters. _____

28. A Cessna 185 flies an average of 208 km in
    one hour. How many meters can the Cessna
    fly in one hour? _____

Name _____

Using Conversion Factors

Convert.

1. 21 feet = _____ inches   **2.** 21 feet = _____ yards

3. 4 miles = _____ feet   **4.** 15 pounds = _____ ounces

5. 36 quarts = _____ gallons   **6.** 252 inches = _____ feet

7. 48 ounces = _____ pounds   **8.** 31 gallons = _____ quarts

9. 35 yards = _____ feet   **10.** 8 quarts = _____ gallons

11. 21,120 feet = _____ miles   **12.** 80 ounces = _____ pounds

13. 63 gallons = _____ quarts   **14.** 32 quarts = _____ gallons

15. 39 feet = _____ yards   **16.** 18 miles = _____ feet

17. 23 gallons = _____ quarts   **18.** 96 ounces = _____ pounds

19. 132 inches = _____ feet   **20.** 71 yards = _____ feet

21. 60 quarts = _____ gallons   **22.** 31 pounds = _____ ounces

23. 63,360 feet = _____ miles   **24.** 47 feet = _____ inches

25. 23 gallons = _____ quarts   **26.** 42 feet = _____ yards

27. 288 ounces = _____ pounds   **28.** 73 miles = _____ feet

29. 84 quarts = _____ gallons   **30.** 46 pounds = _____ ounces

31. 276 inches = _____ feet   **32.** 51 yards = _____ feet

33. 7 gallons = _____ quarts   **34.** 656 ounces = _____ pounds

35. 79,200 feet = _____ miles   **36.** 53 feet = _____ inches

37. 26 pounds = _____ ounces   **38.** 127 miles = _____ feet

39. Science A gray whale can be up to 540 inches in length.
How many feet is that? How many yards? _____

40. In 1986, G. Graham of Edmond, Oklahoma, grew a
pumpkin weighing 7.75 lb. How many ounces is that? _____

Name _____

Section 4A Review

For Exercises 1–5, find the perimeter and give the answer in meters.

1. _____

15 m
8 m
12 m
8 m

2. _____

21 cm
9 cm

3. _____

4 m
8 m
4 m
5 m

4. A square with sides of length 18 km _____

5. A 7-sided figure with all sides 33 mm _____

For Exercises 6–10, find the perimeter and give the answer in feet.

6. _____

12 ft
7 ft
3 ft
16 ft

7. _____

42 in.
20 in.
25 in.

8. _____

4 yd
3 yd
3 yd
6 yd

9. A square with sides of length of 15 yards _____

10. A rectangle with sides of length 2 mi and 5 mi _____

Use the conversion factor to find the missing measurement.

11. 5 kilograms in 5000 grams

_____ kilograms in 8300 grams

12. 5280 feet in 1 mile

19,008 feet in _____ miles

Convert.

13. 18 qt = _____ gal **14.** 700 mL = _____ L **15.** 87 ft = _____ yd

16. A sign at an amusement park says "You must be at least 56 in. tall to ride the Super Swoosh." Roger rounds this to 60 in., or 5 ft, and concludes that he cannot ride since he is only 4 ft 10 in. tall. Do you agree with his reasoning? Explain. *[Lesson 2-2]*

_____

17. Estimate the length of the lizard to the nearest centimeter and tenth of a centimeter. *[Lesson 3-2]*

0   1   2   3   4   5   6
Centimeters

_____

Area of Squares and Rectangles

Find the missing measurement for each rectangle.

1. Area = _____

Base = 7 ft

Height = 9 ft

2. Area = 24 cm^2

Base = _____

Height = 6 cm

3. Area = 84 in^2

Base = 7 in.

Height = _____

4. Area = 11.5 m^2

Base = 5 m

Height = _____

5. Area = _____

Base = 5.875 in.

Height = 4 in.

6. Area = 12.46 cm^2

Base = _____

Height = 7 cm

Find the area of each figure.

7. Square with sides of length 8 ft _____

8. Rectangle with sides 4.7 m and 7.3 m _____

9. Square with sides of length 21 cm _____

10. Rectangle with sides 8.3 m and 5.2 m _____

11. Rectangle with sides 9 in. and 4 in. _____

Use the scatterplot for Exercises 12–14.

12. What is the area of each rectangle?

R _____ S _____ T _____

U _____ V _____ W _____

13. Which rectangle is also a square? _____

14. What is the area of the rectangle
with the greatest height? _____

Rectangles *R–W*

15. Shelly plans to paint a wall in her bedroom. The wall is 11 ft long
and 8 ft high. She needs enough paint to cover how much area? _____

16. In 1993, the Food Bank for Monterey County (California) set
a record by baking a lasagne with an area of 490 ft^2. If the
lasagne was 70 ft long, how wide was it? _____

Name _____

Area of Parallelograms

Find each area. The dashed line is a height.

1. _____

7 cm
4 cm

2. _____

10 yd
12 yd

3. _____

9 km
8 km

4. _____

42 in.
63 in.

5. _____

17 mm
28 mm

6. _____

3.7 ft
7.1 ft

7. _____

6.5
6.3

8. _____

2.3 cm   3.1 cm

9. _____

8.1 in.
11.3 in.

Find the area if b is the base and h is the height of the parallelogram.

10. $b = 5$ cm, $h = 7$ cm

11. $b = 8.6$ m, $h = 12.0$ m

12. $b = 8.4$ m, $h = 5.3$ m

_____   _____   _____

13. $h = 83$ in., $b = 104$ in.

14. $b = 23$ cm, $h = 8.7$ cm

15. $h = 2.1$ mi, $b = 2.5$ mi

_____   _____   _____

16. A woodworker built a table whose top was inlaid with a parallelogram with base 8 in. and height 9.5 in. What was the area of the inlay?

_____

17. An unusual tabletop has the shape of a parallelogram with base 147 cm and height 136 cm. What is the area of the tabletop?

_____

Name _____

Area of Triangles

Find the area of each triangle. The dashed line is a height.

1. _____

18 m, 7 m

2. _____

6 in., 8 in.

3. _____

13 cm, 11 cm

4. _____

8.1, 24.8

5. _____

21.36 yd, 18 yd

6. _____

12.9 m, 11.7 m

7. _____

8.3 ft, 7 ft

8. _____

3.2 cm, 5.3 cm

9. _____

7.8 mi, 4.7 mi

Find the area if b is the base and h is the height of the triangle.

10. $b = 12$ ft, $h = 5$ ft

11. $h = 9$ cm, $b = 11$ cm

12. $b = 4.2$ mi, $h = 6$ mi

_____ _____ _____

13. $h = 7.3$, $b = 12.4$

14. $b = 8.37$ in., $h = 10.4$ in. **15.** $h = 2.8$ km, $b = 5.8$ km

_____ _____ _____

16. $b = 9.6$ yd, $h = 6.42$ yd **17.** $h = 20.6$ cm, $b = 6.4$ cm **18.** $b = 3.8$ ft, $h = 9.1$ ft

_____ _____ _____

19. Geography The state of New Hampshire has the
approximate shape of a triangle with base 90 mi and
height 180 mi. Estimate the area of New Hampshire.

_____

Name _____

Section 4B Review

Find the area of each figure.

1. _____

2. _____

3. _____

Find the perimeter of each figure.

4. _____

5. _____

6. _____

7. Rhonda wants to carpet a room measuring 8 ft by 10 ft. She has a piece of carpet measuring 12 ft by 6 ft. Is it possible to cut the carpet into several pieces and assemble a piece large enough to carpet the room? Explain.

_____

_____

8. A board for the game of Chinese checkers has the shape of 12 triangles placed together. If each of the 12 triangles has base 10 cm and height 17.3 cm, what is the area of the board?

_____

9. In 1980, the population of Texas was about 3^{15}. Use a calculator to write this number in standard form. [Lesson 2-4]

_____

10. There are about 4,014,500,000 square inches in a square mile. Write this number in scientific notation. [Lesson 3-4]

_____

Name _____

Name _____

Practice
4-7

Discovering π

Find the circumference. Use 3.14 for π.

1. _____

4 cm

2. _____

5 in.

3. _____

23 m

4. _____

16 ft

5. _____

12 mi

6. _____

33 m

Find the missing measurements for each circle where *r* = radius,
d = diameter, and *c* = circumference.

7. *r* = 8 cm, *d* = 16 cm, *c* = _____

8. *r* = _____, *d* = 28, *c* = 87.92

9. *r* = 16 in., *d* = _____, *c* = 100.48 in.

10. *r* = 2.5 mm, *d* = _____, *c* = _____

11. *r* = 18 cm, *d* = _____, *c* = _____

12. *r* = _____, *d* = 34 mi, *c* = _____

13. *r* = _____, *d* = _____, *c* = 75.36 ft

14. *r* = 10 yd, *d* = _____, *c* = _____

15. *r* = 40 mi, *d* = _____, *c* = _____

16. *r* = _____, *d* = _____, *c* = 11.932

17. A circular track has a circumference of
0.4082 km. Find the diameter of the track.

_____

18. Geometry The radius of the earth is about 3960 mi.
Estimate the length of the equator.

_____

Name _____

Area of Circles

Find the area. Use 3.14 for π.

1. _____ **2.** _____ **3.** _____

Find the area of each circle where r = radius and d = diameter.

4. r = 7 in.   **5.** d = 22 cm   **6.** r = 5 mi   **7.** d = 40 m

_____   _____   _____   _____

8. d = 9 yd   **9.** r = 100 km   **10.** d = 75 in.   **11.** r = 62 mm

_____   _____   _____   _____

Given the circumference of a circle, find the radius and the area
rounded to the nearest tenth.

12. c = 43.96 cm   **13.** c = 16.96 in.   **14.** c = 72.22 m   **15.** c = 11.32 yd

r = _____   r = _____   r = _____   r = _____

A = _____   A = _____   A = _____   A = _____

16. c = 229.9 mm   **17.** c = 103 ft   **18.** c = 34.63 km   **19.** c = 25.1 in.

r = _____   r = _____   r = _____   r = _____

A = _____   A = _____   A = _____   A = _____

Use the scatterplot for Exercises 20–22.
Assume all plates are circular.

20. Find the cost of the plate with diameter 13 in. _____

21. Find the radius of the most expensive plate.   _____

22. Which plate has the smallest circumference? _____

23. The diameter of a compact disc is about 12 cm.
Find the approximate area of a compact disc.   _____

Plate Comparison

Area of Irregular Shapes

Find the area of each irregular figure. Use 3.14 for π.

1. _____

2. _____

3. _____

4. _____

5. _____

6. _____

7. _____

8. _____

9. _____

10. _____

11. _____

12. _____

13. Geography Find the approximate area of Nevada.

_____

Name _____

Section 4C Review

Find the area and the distance around the shape.

1. area: _____

distance: _____

2. area: _____

distance: _____

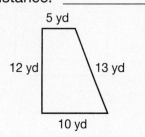

5 yd

12 yd   13 yd

10 yd

3. area: _____

distance: _____

8 km

11 km

7 km

13 km

4. area: _____

distance: _____

9

6

6

15

7

5. area: _____

distance: _____

18 in.

6. area: _____

distance: _____

16 km

15 km

7. area: _____

distance: _____

21 cm

8. area: _____

distance: _____

10 in.   10 in.

6 in.

4 in.   3 in.   4 in.

8 in.

9. area: _____

distance: _____

11 m

10. The table shows a snail's progress as it moves along a telephone pole. Complete the table by assuming that the pattern continues.

Time	Mon. AM	Mon. PM	Tues. AM	Tues. PM	Wed. AM	Wed. PM	Thurs. AM
Height (ft)	6	10	9	13			

11. The lot shown has perimeter 319.8 ft. Write and solve an equation to find the length of the unknown side. *[Lesson 3-7]* _____

103.7 ft

56.2 ft

x

81.3 ft

Main Street

Poplar Avenue

Name _____

Cumulative Review Chapters 1–4

Find the mean of each set of data. *[Lesson 1-8]*

1. 37, 43, 64, 53, 39, 28

2. 635, 842, 963, 612, 385

_____

_____

3. 8, 5, 8, 3, 9, 8, 8, 4, 3, 7

4. 8.6, 12.4, 7.3, 11.2, 13.1, 14.2, 13.0

_____

_____

Estimate. *[Lesson 2-6]*

5. 286 + 541

6. 8,912 – 4,371

7. 305 + 290 + 310 + 286

_____

_____

_____

8. 914 – 352

9. 2,165 + 891

10. 6,140 + 5,912 + 6,041

_____

_____

_____

Round to the underlined place value. *[Lesson 3-2]*

11. 38.4<u>6</u>5

12. 5.<u>8</u>364

13. 2.1<u>7</u>59

14. 14.3<u>7</u>55

_____

_____

_____

_____

15. 5.8<u>1</u>49

16. 6.74<u>3</u>1

17. 2.<u>8</u>65

18. 56.4<u>1</u>3

_____

_____

_____

_____

Convert. *[Lesson 4-3]*

19. 17 feet = _____ inches

20. 32 pounds = _____ ounces

21. 14 miles = _____ feet

22. 136 quarts = _____ gallons

Find the area. *[Lesson 4-5]*

23. _____

24. _____

25. _____

Divisibility

Tell whether the number is divisible by 2, 3, 5, 6, 9, or 10.

1. 75

2. 532

3. 625

4. 39

_____ _____ _____ _____

5. 118

6. 354

7. 585

8. 408

_____ _____ _____ _____

9. 235

10. 105

11. 186

12. 73

_____ _____ _____ _____

13. 69

14. 317

15. 200

16. 366

_____ _____ _____ _____

17. 306

18. 645

19. 223

20. 326

_____ _____ _____ _____

Tell whether the first number is divisible by the second.

21. 46, 7 _____ **22.** 65, 2 _____ **23.** 43, 10 _____ **24.** 165, 3 _____

25. 133, 5 _____ **26.** 66, 11 _____ **27.** 85, 3 _____ **28.** 185, 5 _____

29. 99, 6 _____ **30.** 106, 7 _____ **31.** 150, 3 _____ **32.** 196, 2 _____

33. 99, 5 _____ **34.** 128, 4 _____ **35.** 39, 6 _____ **36.** 33, 3 _____

37. 110, 6 _____ **38.** 129, 9 _____ **39.** 37, 5 _____ **40.** 126, 7 _____

41. 117, 8 _____ **42.** 96, 8 _____ **43.** 63, 2 _____ **44.** 192, 10 _____

45. 74, 4 _____ **46.** 55, 5 _____ **47.** 171, 8 _____ **48.** 165, 11 _____

49. There are 365 days in a non-leap year.
Test 365 for divisibility by 2, 3, 5, 6, and 10. _____

50. Social Science During an election year, the
U.S. President is chosen by 538 electoral votes.
Test 538 for divisibility by 2, 3, 5, 6, and 10. _____

Prime Factorization

Given the number and its factors, tell whether it is prime or composite.

1. 92: 1, 2, 4, 23, 46, 92

2. 121: 1, 11, 121

3. 83: 1, 83

_____

_____

_____

4. 129: 1, 3, 43, 129

5. 52: 1, 2, 4, 13, 26, 52

6. 55: 1, 5, 11, 55

_____

_____

_____

7. 29: 1, 29

8. 57: 1, 3, 19, 57

9. 63: 1, 3, 7, 9, 21, 63

_____

_____

_____

Find the prime factorization.

10. 12

11. 40

12. 64

_____

_____

_____

13. 36

14. 60

15. 65

_____

_____

_____

16. 20

17. 30

18. 56

_____

_____

_____

19. 21

20. 18

21. 16

_____

_____

_____

22. 630

23. 1001

24. 625

_____

_____

_____

25. The prime factorization of a number is
$2 \times 2 \times 3 \times 3 \times 3 \times 5 \times 5 \times 5 \times 5 \times 5$.
What is the number?

_____

26. Social Science The House of Representatives has
435 members. If a committee has a prime number of
members, and that number is a factor of 435, then how
many members can be on the committee?

Least Common Multiples

List the first three common multiples of the given numbers.

1. 3, 2   **2.** 3, 4   **3.** 5, 4   **4.** 2, 8

_____   _____   _____   _____

5. 3, 5   **6.** 2, 7   **7.** 6, 5   **8.** 13, 2

_____   _____   _____   _____

Find the LCM of each pair.

9. 6, 23 _____ **10.** 3, 21 _____ **11.** 9, 5 _____ **12.** 17, 3 _____

13. 7, 5 _____ **14.** 21, 7 _____ **15.** 2, 12 _____ **16.** 15, 11 _____

17. 4, 19 _____ **18.** 6, 28 _____ **19.** 14, 18 _____ **20.** 23, 2 _____

21. 15, 14 _____ **22.** 11, 33 _____ **23.** 5, 15 _____ **24.** 8, 5 _____

25. 26, 22 _____ **26.** 3, 22 _____ **27.** 2, 34 _____ **28.** 15, 8 _____

29. 10, 15 _____ **30.** 12, 4 _____ **31.** 6, 10 _____ **32.** 43, 13 _____

33. 24, 3 _____ **34.** 36, 45 _____ **35.** 17, 2 _____ **36.** 24, 7 _____

37. 29, 5 _____ **38.** 27, 2 _____ **39.** 9, 10 _____ **40.** 31, 5 _____

41. 62, 9 _____ **42.** 2, 7 _____ **43.** 6, 4 _____ **44.** 10, 2 _____

45. 4, 10 _____ **46.** 6, 11 _____ **47.** 11, 2 _____ **48.** 7, 12 _____

49. 7, 16 _____ **50.** 16, 6 _____ **51.** 10, 14 _____ **52.** 22, 4 _____

53. Marti works Monday through Saturday, so she has a day
off once every 7 days. She needs to give her dog some
medicine every 5 days. How often does she give her dog
medicine on her day off?   _____

54. The traffic signal at 4th and Main turns green every 6 minutes.
The signal at 5th and Broadway turns green every 4 minutes.
If both turned green at 12:15 P.M., when are the next three
times that both will turn green at the same time?

_____

Section 5A Review

Tell whether the first number is divisible by the second.

1. 95, 5 _____   **2.** 72, 6 _____   **3.** 38, 4 _____   **4.** 48, 9 _____

Find the prime factorization.

5. 85 _____   **6.** 72 _____   **7.** 220 _____

8. 231 _____   **9.** 128 _____   **10.** 148 _____

List the first seven multiples of the number.

11. 3   **12.** 11

_____   _____

13. 8   **14.** 60

_____   _____

Find the LCM of each pair.

15. 2, 9 _____   **16.** 15, 10 _____   **17.** 7, 63 _____   **18.** 22, 4 _____

19. A certain city holds elections for mayor in years divisible by 3. These elections will be held in which years between 1996 and 2015?

_____

20. Margo's locker combination consists of the first three even multiples of 9, in order. What is her combination? _____

21. The prime factorization of a number is $5 \times 7 \times 7 \times 17$. What is the number? _____

22. Health A serving of stir fried mung bean sprouts has 3 times as much iron as a serving of boiled mung bean sprouts. The stir fried sprouts have 2.4 mg of iron. Write and solve an equation to find the amount of iron in a serving of boiled bean sprouts. *[Lesson 3-12]*

_____

23. A certain brand of washing machine uses 140 liters of water to do a load of laundry. Convert this amount to milliliters. *[Lesson 4-2]* _____

Understanding Fractions

For each fraction, draw a model and name an equivalent fraction.

1. $\frac{1}{3}$ _____

2. $\frac{3}{5}$ _____

3. $\frac{8}{12}$ _____

4. $\frac{5}{7}$ _____

5. $\frac{5}{9}$ _____

6. $\frac{8}{20}$ _____

7. $\frac{15}{25}$ _____

8. $\frac{2}{5}$ _____

9. $\frac{1}{6}$ _____

10. $\frac{5}{6}$ _____

11. $\frac{1}{10}$ _____

12. $\frac{3}{6}$ _____

The picture shows how to set up the game of backgammon.
The 24 triangular-shaped spaces on the board are called points.

13. What fraction of the points have
    white playing pieces? _____

14. What fraction of the points have
    five black playing pieces? _____

15. What fraction of the white playing
    pieces are on the point shown at
    the upper left corner of the board? _____

16. Arturo has 3 dogs and 5 cats. What
    fraction of his pets are dogs? _____

Fractions in Lowest Terms

Find two fractions equivalent to each fraction.

1. $\frac{8}{10}$ _____ **2.** $\frac{3}{4}$ _____ **3.** $\frac{8}{24}$ _____

4. $\frac{4}{7}$ _____ **5.** $\frac{18}{21}$ _____ **6.** $\frac{6}{8}$ _____

7. $\frac{12}{14}$ _____ **8.** $\frac{5}{9}$ _____ **9.** $\frac{6}{9}$ _____

10. $\frac{6}{14}$ _____ **11.** $\frac{12}{30}$ _____ **12.** $\frac{4}{13}$ _____

Write in lowest terms.

13. $\frac{12}{24}$ _____ **14.** $\frac{6}{9}$ _____ **15.** $\frac{9}{21}$ _____ **16.** $\frac{8}{10}$ _____

17. $\frac{6}{28}$ _____ **18.** $\frac{18}{20}$ _____ **19.** $\frac{30}{38}$ _____ **20.** $\frac{8}{20}$ _____

21. $\frac{12}{18}$ _____ **22.** $\frac{14}{32}$ _____ **23.** $\frac{8}{12}$ _____ **24.** $\frac{12}{16}$ _____

25. $\frac{12}{30}$ _____ **26.** $\frac{9}{15}$ _____ **27.** $\frac{6}{42}$ _____ **28.** $\frac{9}{12}$ _____

29. $\frac{6}{15}$ _____ **30.** $\frac{6}{10}$ _____ **31.** $\frac{6}{12}$ _____ **32.** $\frac{24}{30}$ _____

Find the GCF of each pair.

33. 16, 10 _____ **34.** 11, 18 _____ **35.** 15, 6 _____ **36.** 8, 6 _____

37. 3, 6 _____ **38.** 20, 15 _____ **39.** 12, 18 _____ **40.** 3, 14 _____

41. 8, 12 _____ **42.** 10, 14 _____ **43.** 21, 15 _____ **44.** 49, 70 _____

45. 36, 60 _____ **46.** 70, 42 _____ **47.** 32, 76 _____ **48.** 64, 4 _____

49. 15, 75 _____ **50.** 63, 42 _____ **51.** 30, 65 _____ **52.** 32, 24 _____

53. Measurement A kilometer is about $\frac{6}{10}$ of a mile.
Write this distance in lowest terms. _____

54. $\frac{25}{30}$ of the students in Mrs. Lim's class went on last
week's field trip. Write this fraction in lowest terms. _____

Improper Fractions and
Mixed Numbers

Write each mixed number as an improper fraction.

1. $2\frac{1}{6}$ _____ **2.** $5\frac{1}{5}$ _____ **3.** $1\frac{2}{5}$ _____ **4.** $13\frac{1}{2}$ _____

5. $8\frac{3}{4}$ _____ **6.** $3\frac{2}{3}$ _____ **7.** $1\frac{3}{5}$ _____ **8.** $4\frac{1}{2}$ _____

9. $14\frac{2}{9}$ _____ **10.** $12\frac{2}{3}$ _____ **11.** $3\frac{5}{8}$ _____ **12.** $9\frac{1}{9}$ _____

13. $5\frac{2}{3}$ _____ **14.** $7\frac{4}{5}$ _____ **15.** $8\frac{1}{3}$ _____ **16.** $4\frac{3}{4}$ _____

Write each improper fraction as a mixed number.

17. $\frac{17}{4}$ _____ **18.** $\frac{19}{2}$ _____ **19.** $\frac{37}{3}$ _____ **20.** $\frac{16}{7}$ _____

21. $\frac{32}{3}$ _____ **22.** $\frac{77}{8}$ _____ **23.** $\frac{101}{7}$ _____ **24.** $\frac{33}{4}$ _____

25. $\frac{27}{2}$ _____ **26.** $\frac{19}{3}$ _____ **27.** $\frac{41}{9}$ _____ **28.** $\frac{61}{6}$ _____

29. $\frac{59}{10}$ _____ **30.** $\frac{19}{4}$ _____ **31.** $\frac{5}{3}$ _____ **32.** $\frac{26}{5}$ _____

Science Write the mixed number as an improper fraction
or the improper fraction as a mixed number.

33. A geranosaurus was $1\frac{1}{5}$ m long. _____

34. Each arm of a deinocherius was $\frac{17}{2}$ ft long. _____

35. A hypsilophodon was $\frac{23}{10}$ m long. _____

36. A protoceratops was $\frac{9}{5}$ m long. _____

37. An anatosaurus was $13\frac{2}{3}$ m long. _____

38. Heidi built a fort with a ceiling that was $\frac{21}{4}$ ft high. Marvin is
$5\frac{3}{4}$ ft tall. Can Marvin stand up straight in Heidi's fort? _____

Converting Fractions and Decimals

Rewrite using bar notation.

1. 0.77777777 ... _____   **2.** 0.58585858 ... _____   **3.** 2.65656565 ... _____

4. 3.008008008 ... _____   **5.** 4.876767676 ... _____   **6.** 12.12121212 ... _____

7. 4.93333333 ... _____   **8.** 7.50505050 ... _____   **9.** 6.80888888 ... _____

Write each fraction as a decimal. State whether the decimal terminates or repeats.

10. $\frac{2}{3}$ _____   **11.** $\frac{7}{10}$ _____   **12.** $\frac{3}{5}$ _____   **13.** $\frac{15}{6}$ _____

_____   _____   _____   _____

14. $\frac{23}{33}$ _____   **15.** $\frac{1}{8}$ _____   **16.** $\frac{5}{11}$ _____   **17.** $\frac{36}{25}$ _____

_____   _____   _____   _____

18. $\frac{41}{100}$ _____   **19.** $\frac{5}{6}$ _____   **20.** $\frac{21}{40}$ _____   **21.** $\frac{49}{50}$ _____

_____   _____   _____   _____

Write each decimal as a fraction in lowest terms.

22. 0.25 _____   **23.** 0.74 _____   **24.** 0.5 _____   **25.** 0.47 _____

26. 0.8 _____   **27.** 0.375 _____   **28.** 0.515 _____   **29.** 0.863 _____

30. 0.28 _____   **31.** 0.45 _____   **32.** 0.7 _____   **33.** 0.186 _____

34. 0.504 _____   **35.** 0.84 _____   **36.** 0.775 _____   **37.** 0.868 _____

38. Measurement Gilbert is using a set of drill bits that came in the following sizes: 0.0625 in., 0.125 in., 0.1875 in., 0.25 in., and 0.375 in. Write each drill bit size as a fraction in lowest terms.

_____

39. Technology A computer word processing program allows users to select a font size of 8 pt, 10 pt, 12 pt, or 16 pt. These sizes are equivalent to $\frac{1}{9}$ in., $\frac{5}{36}$ in., $\frac{1}{6}$ in., and $\frac{2}{9}$ in., respectively. Write each font size as a decimal.

_____

Name _____

Comparing and Ordering

Compare using $<$, $>$, or $=$.

1. $\frac{1}{4}\bigcirc\frac{4}{13}$ 2. $\frac{2}{4}\bigcirc\frac{10}{20}$ 3. $\frac{5}{7}\bigcirc\frac{6}{7}$ 4. $\frac{5}{12}\bigcirc\frac{3}{5}$

5. $\frac{2}{9}\bigcirc\frac{1}{5}$ 6. $\frac{1}{7}\bigcirc\frac{3}{18}$ 7. $\frac{4}{9}\bigcirc\frac{3}{7}$ 8. $\frac{12}{18}\bigcirc\frac{10}{14}$

9. $\frac{12}{16}\bigcirc\frac{4}{6}$ 10. $\frac{7}{20}\bigcirc\frac{1}{3}$ 11. $\frac{2}{8}\bigcirc\frac{3}{15}$ 12. $\frac{2}{6}\bigcirc\frac{4}{12}$

13. $\frac{2}{5}\bigcirc\frac{5}{11}$ 14. $\frac{10}{16}\bigcirc\frac{3}{4}$ 15. $\frac{7}{11}\bigcirc\frac{9}{13}$ 16. $\frac{2}{7}\bigcirc\frac{2}{9}$

Order from smallest to largest.

17. $\frac{3}{8}, \frac{3}{9}, \frac{3}{10}$ 18. $\frac{4}{5}, \frac{5}{4}, \frac{4}{4}$ 19. $\frac{7}{10}, \frac{18}{25}, \frac{3}{5}$

_____ _____ _____

20. $\frac{3}{4}, \frac{2}{5}, \frac{11}{20}$ 21. $\frac{2}{3}, \frac{3}{4}, \frac{5}{6}$ 22. $\frac{7}{15}, \frac{1}{3}, \frac{2}{5}$

_____ _____ _____

23. $\frac{1}{5}, \frac{1}{6}, \frac{7}{30}$ 24. $\frac{6}{11}, \frac{3}{7}, \frac{4}{9}$ 25. $\frac{1}{2}, \frac{2}{5}, \frac{1}{3}$

_____ _____ _____

26. $\frac{5}{8}, \frac{3}{4}, \frac{7}{10}$ 27. $\frac{33}{100}, \frac{3}{10}, \frac{33}{1000}$ 28. $\frac{40}{49}, \frac{13}{28}, \frac{3}{14}$

_____ _____ _____

29. **Measurement** Ralph has $2\frac{1}{3}$ cups of milk. Does
he have enough to prepare a recipe that uses $2\frac{1}{2}$ cups? _____

30. **Measurement** Jody's Hardware stocks wooden dowels in
the following widths: $\frac{3}{16}$ in., $\frac{1}{8}$ in., $\frac{3}{8}$ in., $\frac{1}{4}$ in., $\frac{1}{2}$ in. Write these
widths in order from the least to the greatest.

_____

Name _____

Section 5B Review

Determine what fraction the shaded part represents.
Identify the numerator and denominator of each fraction.

1. fraction: _____

   numerator: _____

   denominator: _____

2. fraction: _____

   numerator: _____

   denominator: _____

3. fraction: _____

   numerator: _____

   denominator: _____

4. fraction: _____

   numerator: _____

   denominator: _____

Write each fraction in lowest terms and as a decimal.

5. $\frac{16}{20}$ **6.** $\frac{6}{16}$ **7.** $\frac{8}{24}$ **8.** $\frac{21}{42}$

_____   _____   _____   _____

9. $\frac{84}{100}$ **10.** $\frac{9}{36}$ **11.** $\frac{10}{12}$ **12.** $\frac{45}{72}$

_____   _____   _____   _____

Write each mixed number as an improper fraction or the improper fraction as a mixed number.

13. $3\frac{5}{6}$ _____   **14.** $\frac{23}{5}$ _____   **15.** $7\frac{3}{8}$ _____   **16.** $\frac{47}{10}$ _____

17. Fred and Gina are baking cookies. Fred puts chocolate icing on every eighth cookie, and Gina puts colored sprinkles on every fifth cookie. Which cookies have both chocolate icing and colored sprinkles? _____

18. Bill correctly answered $\frac{3}{14}$ of the problems on an algebra test. Cheryl correctly answered $\frac{1}{7}$ of the problems, and Dana correctly answered $\frac{1}{4}$ of the problems. Order these students from the fewest correct answers to the most. _____

19. A store owner obtained a compact stereo system for $86.72 and sold it for $97.95. What was the profit? *[Lesson 3-1]* _____

20. Science A king salmon can weigh up to 100 pounds or more. How many ounces is that? *[Lesson 4-3]* _____

Name _____

Cumulative Review Chapters 1–5

Order each group of numbers from least to greatest.
[Lesson 2-3]

1. 3,333; 33,333; 333

2. 60,660; 60,606; 66,006

_____   _____

3. 7,000; 7,010; 7,009; 6,999

4. 5 billion; 4 million; 6 hundred

_____   _____

Simplify. *[Lessons 3-6 and 3-11]*

5. $8.37 + 21$ **6.** $5.43 - 1.9$ **7.** $6.98 + 7.47$ **8.** $12 - 5.63$

_____   _____   _____   _____

9. $24.893 \div 3.1$ **10.** $4.36 + 8.9$ **11.** $1.4535 \div 0.085$ **12.** $0.828 \div 3.6$

_____   _____   _____   _____

Find the missing measurement for each rectangle. *[Lesson 4-4]*

13. Area = 66 in^2

Base = _____

Height= 6 in.

14. Area = _____

Base = 6 ft

Height = 15 ft

15. Area = 35 m^2

Base = 5 m

Height = _____

16. Area = 48 km^2

Base = 12 km

Height = _____

17. Area = _____

Base = 6.5 yd

Height = 4.1 yd

18. Area = 9.25 mm^2

Base = _____

Height = 2.5 mm

Find the prime factorization. *[Lesson 5-2]*

19. 350 _____

20. 135 _____

21. 616 _____

22. 180 _____

Write as a fraction in lowest terms *[Lesson 5-7]*

23. 0.625 _____   **24.** 0.47 _____   **25.** 0.775 _____   **26.** 0.42 _____

Adding and Subtracting Fractions with Like Denominators

Simplify. Write each answer in lowest terms.

1. $\frac{3}{20} - \frac{1}{20}$ ——

2. $\frac{6}{15} + \frac{4}{15}$ ——

3. $\frac{3}{4} + \frac{3}{4}$ ——

4. $\frac{6}{8} + \frac{3}{8}$ ——

5. $\frac{2}{13} + \frac{3}{13}$ ——

6. $\frac{6}{8} - \frac{5}{8}$ ——

7. $\frac{3}{15} + \frac{10}{15}$ ——

8. $\frac{8}{10} - \frac{4}{10}$ ——

9. $\frac{7}{14} - \frac{3}{14}$ ——

10. $\frac{1}{4} + \frac{1}{4}$ ——

11. $\frac{6}{7} - \frac{1}{7}$ ——

12. $\frac{14}{19} - \frac{5}{19}$ ——

13. $\frac{5}{6} + \frac{5}{6}$ ——

14. $\frac{2}{3} + \frac{1}{3}$ ——

15. $\frac{15}{18} + \frac{4}{18}$ ——

16. $\frac{10}{15} - \frac{6}{15}$ ——

State whether the answer is greater than, less than, or equal to 1.

17. $\frac{7}{11} - \frac{3}{11}$

18. $\frac{4}{10} + \frac{6}{10}$

19. $\frac{2}{4} + \frac{3}{4}$

_____

_____

_____

20. $\frac{1}{4} + \frac{2}{4}$

21. $\frac{5}{6} - \frac{1}{6}$

22. $\frac{2}{5} + \frac{4}{5}$

_____

_____

_____

Each guest at Tony's 8th birthday party brought one gift or a card. The bar graph shows the gifts that Tony received. Use the graph for Exercises 23–25.

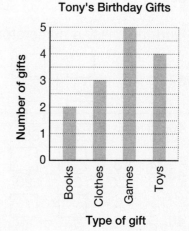

Tony's Birthday Gifts

23. What fraction of the gifts were books or games? _____

24. What fraction of the gifts were clothing, games, or toys? _____

25. There were 18 guests at the party. What fraction brought cards only? _____

26. In 1990, about $\frac{1}{8}$ of the American population was of age 65 or older. What fraction of the population was under 65? _____

27. In 1993, $\frac{11}{20}$ of America's electricity was produced using coal, and $\frac{4}{20}$ of America's electricity was produced using nuclear power. What fraction was produced using other means such as natural gas or hydroelectric power? _____

Adding and Subtracting Fractions with Unlike Denominators

Simplify. Write each answer in lowest terms.

1. $\frac{3}{5} - \frac{1}{3}$ _____

2. $\frac{1}{2} + \frac{7}{22}$ _____

3. $\frac{9}{16} - \frac{1}{8}$ _____

4. $\frac{3}{5} - \frac{4}{9}$ _____

5. $\frac{1}{5} - \frac{1}{7}$ _____

6. $\frac{11}{24} + \frac{1}{3}$ _____

7. $\frac{1}{3} - \frac{1}{10}$ _____

8. $\frac{7}{10} - \frac{3}{5}$ _____

9. $\frac{8}{9} - \frac{7}{12}$ _____

10. $\frac{5}{6} - \frac{1}{2}$ _____

11. $\frac{7}{10} + \frac{2}{25}$ _____

12. $\frac{4}{5} + \frac{1}{10}$ _____

13. $\frac{5}{8} - \frac{1}{3}$ _____

14. $\frac{1}{6} + \frac{9}{16}$ _____

15. $\frac{1}{2} + \frac{5}{11}$ _____

16. $\frac{1}{6} + \frac{17}{24}$ _____

17. $\frac{1}{7} + \frac{2}{3}$ _____

18. $\frac{1}{5} + \frac{3}{5}$ _____

19. $\frac{1}{7} - \frac{1}{9}$ _____

20. $\frac{5}{7} - \frac{1}{2}$ _____

21. $\frac{1}{2} - \frac{5}{11}$ _____

22. $\frac{1}{9} + \frac{2}{3}$ _____

23. $\frac{1}{4} - \frac{1}{11}$ _____

24. $\frac{5}{13} + \frac{2}{5}$ _____

25. $\frac{5}{6} - \frac{4}{15}$ _____

26. $\frac{13}{14} - \frac{1}{2}$ _____

27. $\frac{7}{8} - \frac{1}{2}$ _____

28. $\frac{1}{4} + \frac{3}{10}$ _____

29. $\frac{1}{5} - \frac{1}{13}$ _____

30. $\frac{1}{5} + \frac{1}{6}$ _____

31. $\frac{2}{7} + \frac{1}{3}$ _____

32. $\frac{6}{25} - \frac{1}{10}$ _____

33. $\frac{14}{15} - \frac{2}{3}$ _____

34. $\frac{14}{15} - \frac{7}{10}$ _____

35. $\frac{4}{5} + \frac{1}{25}$ _____

36. $\frac{1}{6} + \frac{3}{10}$ _____

Find the missing numerators.

37. $\frac{5}{6} + \frac{4}{7} = \frac{\boxed{}}{42} + \frac{\boxed{}}{42}$

38. $\frac{1}{5} - \frac{1}{14} = \frac{\boxed{}}{70} - \frac{\boxed{}}{70}$

39. $\frac{3}{4} - \frac{5}{9} = \frac{\boxed{}}{36} - \frac{\boxed{}}{36}$

40. $\frac{3}{5} + \frac{3}{7} = \frac{\boxed{}}{35} + \frac{\boxed{}}{35}$

41. $\frac{4}{9} - \frac{2}{5} = \frac{\boxed{}}{45} - \frac{\boxed{}}{45}$

42. $\frac{1}{8} + \frac{5}{6} = \frac{\boxed{}}{24} + \frac{\boxed{}}{24}$

43. $\frac{4}{5} - \frac{3}{20} = \frac{\boxed{}}{20} - \frac{\boxed{}}{20}$

44. $\frac{2}{3} - \frac{1}{15} = \frac{\boxed{}}{15} - \frac{\boxed{}}{15}$

45. $\frac{4}{9} + \frac{1}{3} = \frac{\boxed{}}{9} + \frac{\boxed{}}{9}$

46. $\frac{5}{6} - \frac{2}{15} = \frac{\boxed{}}{30} - \frac{\boxed{}}{30}$

47. $\frac{1}{4} + \frac{3}{7} = \frac{\boxed{}}{28} + \frac{\boxed{}}{28}$

48. $\frac{5}{6} - \frac{3}{4} = \frac{\boxed{}}{12} - \frac{\boxed{}}{12}$

49. Randy spends $\frac{1}{3}$ of his week sleeping and $\frac{5}{21}$ of his week working. What fraction of the week is left for other activities? _____

50. **Geography** The three states with the largest areas are Alaska ($\frac{4}{25}$ of U.S. area), Texas ($\frac{2}{27}$ of U.S. area), and California ($\frac{2}{45}$ of U.S. area). What fraction of U.S. area do these states make up altogether? _____

Solving Fraction Equations: Addition and Subtraction

Solve. Write each answer in lowest terms.

1. $\frac{5}{17} + a = \frac{8}{17}$ **2.** $\frac{2}{7} + g = \frac{5}{7}$ **3.** $u - \frac{1}{2} = \frac{1}{10}$ **4.** $\frac{7}{8} - v = \frac{13}{16}$

$a =$ _____ $g =$ _____ $u =$ _____ $v =$ _____

5. $\frac{4}{7} - w = \frac{6}{35}$ **6.** $n - \frac{1}{5} = \frac{3}{10}$ **7.** $f + \frac{7}{22} = \frac{13}{22}$ **8.** $\frac{7}{9} - a = \frac{1}{36}$

$w =$ _____ $n =$ _____ $f =$ _____ $a =$ _____

9. $z - \frac{1}{6} = \frac{1}{6}$ **10.** $g + \frac{1}{4} = \frac{7}{16}$ **11.** $\frac{5}{6} + w = \frac{17}{18}$ **12.** $\frac{3}{8} - f = \frac{1}{24}$

$z =$ _____ $g =$ _____ $w =$ _____ $f =$ _____

Write a true equation using the fractions given.

13. $\frac{3}{5}, \frac{1}{3}, \frac{14}{15}$ **14.** $\frac{12}{35}, \frac{1}{7}, \frac{1}{5}$ **15.** $\frac{5}{8}, \frac{3}{4}, \frac{1}{8}$ **16.** $\frac{1}{12}, \frac{3}{20}, \frac{1}{15}$

_____   _____   _____   _____

17. $\frac{3}{8}, \frac{15}{16}, \frac{9}{16}$ **18.** $\frac{6}{7}, \frac{5}{7}, \frac{1}{7}$ **19.** $\frac{2}{3}, \frac{1}{7}, \frac{17}{21}$ **20.** $\frac{5}{12}, \frac{1}{4}, \frac{2}{3}$

_____   _____   _____   _____

21. $\frac{3}{5}, \frac{1}{2}, \frac{1}{10}$ **22.** $\frac{1}{7}, \frac{3}{4}, \frac{25}{28}$ **23.** $\frac{13}{15}, \frac{1}{5}, \frac{2}{3}$ **24.** $\frac{7}{10}, \frac{9}{20}, \frac{1}{4}$

_____   _____   _____   _____

Write and solve an equation for the given situation.

25. Lori and Fraz ate $\frac{7}{12}$ of a pizza. If Lori ate $\frac{1}{3}$ of the pizza, how much of it did Fraz eat?

_____

26. Irene's gas tank was $\frac{9}{10}$ full when she left her house, and it was $\frac{7}{15}$ full when she arrived for her vacation. What fraction of a tank of gas did she use driving there?

_____

Section 6A Review

Simplify. Write each answer in lowest terms.

1. $\frac{12}{15} - \frac{1}{15}$ _____

2. $\frac{11}{20} + \frac{7}{20}$ _____

3. $\frac{2}{3} - \frac{1}{3}$ _____

4. $\frac{4}{6} - \frac{2}{6}$ _____

5. $\frac{6}{11} - \frac{2}{11}$ _____

6. $\frac{4}{7} - \frac{1}{7}$ _____

7. $\frac{12}{13} + \frac{6}{13}$ _____

8. $\frac{18}{20} - \frac{3}{20}$ _____

9. $\frac{1}{3} + \frac{3}{7}$ _____

10. $\frac{1}{10} + \frac{1}{2}$ _____

11. $\frac{1}{2} + \frac{1}{3}$ _____

12. $\frac{21}{25} - \frac{1}{2}$ _____

13. $\frac{6}{7} - \frac{3}{4}$ _____

14. $\frac{5}{7} - \frac{1}{3}$ _____

15. $\frac{1}{2} + \frac{3}{8}$ _____

16. $\frac{3}{10} - \frac{1}{8}$ _____

17. $\frac{2}{3} - \frac{1}{6}$ _____

18. $\frac{3}{5} + \frac{1}{3}$ _____

19. $\frac{1}{2} + \frac{1}{6}$ _____

20. $\frac{2}{3} + \frac{1}{8}$ _____

21. **Career** Lorenzo's job consists of filing, typing, and answering telephones. He spends $\frac{1}{6}$ of his time filing and $\frac{5}{8}$ of his time typing. What fraction of his time does he spend answering telephones? _____

22. About $\frac{1}{6}$ of Rhode Island's population lives in Providence, and $\frac{1}{12}$ of the state's population lives in Warwick. What fraction of the state's population lives in these two cities combined? _____

Solve.

23. $k - \frac{5}{11} = \frac{1}{22}$

24. $\frac{7}{10} - s = \frac{1}{30}$

25. $f - \frac{3}{4} = \frac{1}{36}$

26. $c + \frac{2}{3} = \frac{23}{30}$

$k =$ _____ $s =$ _____ $f =$ _____ $c =$ _____

27. $\frac{5}{7} - d = \frac{13}{21}$

28. $\frac{1}{6} + p = \frac{13}{30}$

29. $\frac{1}{5} + c = \frac{2}{5}$

30. $w + \frac{17}{20} = \frac{14}{15}$

$d =$ _____ $p =$ _____ $c =$ _____ $w =$ _____

31. The largest maze ever created had the shape of a rectangle with base 500 ft and height 252 ft. Find the area of the maze. *[Lesson 4-4]* _____

32. Beth and Carlos are riding on two different Ferris wheels at the park. Beth's Ferris wheel rotates once every 90 seconds, and Carlos' Ferris wheel rotates once every 75 seconds. If Beth and Carlos are both at the bottom of the wheel now, when is the next time they will both be at the bottom? _____

Estimation: Sums and Differences
of Mixed Numbers

Round to the nearest whole number.

1. $2\frac{4}{5}$ _____   **2.** $11\frac{13}{24}$ _____   **3.** $19\frac{19}{36}$ _____   **4.** $9\frac{21}{34}$ _____

5. $2\frac{1}{9}$ _____   **6.** $8\frac{4}{11}$ _____   **7.** $15\frac{1}{2}$ _____   **8.** $17\frac{5}{21}$ _____

9. $9\frac{5}{9}$ _____   **10.** $4\frac{4}{5}$ _____   **11.** $5\frac{7}{20}$ _____   **12.** $2\frac{2}{9}$ _____

13. $6\frac{8}{23}$ _____   **14.** $3\frac{1}{7}$ _____   **15.** $6\frac{1}{2}$ _____   **16.** $13\frac{6}{7}$ _____

Estimate.

17. $1\frac{1}{7} + 6\frac{5}{6}$ _____   **18.** $9\frac{7}{24} - 7\frac{5}{6}$ _____   **19.** $19\frac{4}{7} + 7\frac{1}{3}$ _____

20. $14\frac{4}{5} + 1\frac{3}{8}$ _____   **21.** $20\frac{1}{15} - 15\frac{2}{5}$ _____   **22.** $4\frac{1}{30} + 2\frac{5}{6} + 3\frac{5}{7}$ _____

23. $7\frac{1}{2} + 6\frac{5}{6}$ _____   **24.** $4\frac{2}{5} + 2\frac{7}{10}$ _____   **25.** $12\frac{17}{18} - 1\frac{1}{2}$ _____

26. $16\frac{5}{8} - 2\frac{1}{2}$ _____   **27.** $9\frac{2}{3} + 3\frac{7}{8} + 4\frac{1}{3}$ _____   **28.** $6\frac{8}{15} - 1\frac{1}{3}$ _____

29. $11\frac{7}{24} + 10\frac{1}{12}$ _____   **30.** $5\frac{3}{8} + 1\frac{11}{24}$ _____   **31.** $11\frac{2}{9} + 4\frac{4}{9} + 8\frac{1}{7}$ _____

32. $3\frac{1}{2} + 9\frac{10}{17}$ _____   **33.** $3\frac{23}{24} - 1\frac{1}{3}$ _____   **34.** $12\frac{22}{25} - 11\frac{4}{5}$ _____

35. $7\frac{1}{20} - 4\frac{9}{20}$ _____   **36.** $1\frac{1}{3} + 14\frac{2}{3}$ _____   **37.** $9\frac{5}{18} - 4\frac{1}{2}$ _____

38. $23\frac{23}{24} - 21\frac{3}{8}$ _____   **39.** $1\frac{7}{12} + 9\frac{1}{6}$ _____   **40.** $11\frac{5}{16} + 11\frac{1}{2}$ _____

41. $6\frac{8}{23} + 5\frac{2}{23}$ _____   **42.** $9\frac{1}{2} + 8\frac{10}{11}$ _____   **43.** $5\frac{5}{9} + 5\frac{1}{2}$ _____

44. $20\frac{23}{30} - 8\frac{3}{5}$ _____   **45.** $24\frac{3}{5} - 17\frac{17}{20}$ _____   **46.** $12\frac{1}{2} + 3\frac{3}{7} + 2\frac{8}{9}$ _____

47. $15\frac{7}{12} + 11\frac{5}{8}$ _____   **48.** $2\frac{2}{7} + 1\frac{5}{6}$ _____   **49.** $19\frac{2}{5} + 5\frac{7}{9}$ _____

50. Bob's punch bowl holds 9 cups. He plans to make a punch using $7\frac{1}{3}$ cups of water and $2\frac{1}{2}$ cups of juice concentrate. Does he need a larger bowl? _____

51. On Monday, Stephanie bought some stock for $\$36\frac{5}{8}$ per share. Her stock went up 2 on Tuesday, up $1\frac{1}{4}$ on Wednesday, up $3\frac{9}{16}$ on Thursday, and was unchanged on Friday. Estimate the price on Friday. _____

Adding Mixed Numbers

Add. Write the answer as a whole or mixed number in lowest terms.

1. $13\frac{1}{5} + 5\frac{3}{5}$ _____

2. $7\frac{2}{5} + 1\frac{2}{3}$ _____

3. $9\frac{20}{23} + 14$ _____

4. $6 + 14\frac{1}{2}$ _____

5. $4 + 9\frac{5}{17}$ _____

6. $3\frac{16}{19} + 7$ _____

7. $10\frac{13}{15} + 4\frac{13}{15}$ _____

8. $2 + 16\frac{5}{19}$ _____

9. $6\frac{1}{7} + 19\frac{2}{5}$ _____

10. $15\frac{1}{2} + 17\frac{1}{7}$ _____

11. $22\frac{1}{6} + 10\frac{4}{5}$ _____

12. $10\frac{1}{4} + 7\frac{3}{4}$ _____

13. $1\frac{4}{5} + 3\frac{5}{6}$ _____

14. $11\frac{10}{11} + 5$ _____

15. $11\frac{3}{8} + 16\frac{3}{4}$ _____

16. $11\frac{4}{5} + 2\frac{13}{15}$ _____

17. $16\frac{4}{15} + 8\frac{13}{15}$ _____

18. $3\frac{7}{12} + 6\frac{17}{24}$ _____

19. $3\frac{1}{15} + 4\frac{3}{5}$ _____

20. $4\frac{1}{3} + 7\frac{5}{13}$ _____

21. $1\frac{3}{8} + 10$ _____

22. $12\frac{1}{8} + 1\frac{1}{3}$ _____

23. $8\frac{7}{15} + 3\frac{5}{9}$ _____

24. $2\frac{21}{22} + 5\frac{1}{2}$ _____

25. $5\frac{5}{12} + 10\frac{11}{24}$ _____

26. $18 + 8\frac{11}{13}$ _____

27. $3\frac{3}{7} + 1\frac{1}{2}$ _____

Use the table for Exercises 28–30.

U.S. Immigrants, 1820–1993 (millions)				
Europe	Asia	North America, Central America	South America	Africa, Oceania, Other
$37\frac{11}{20}$	$7\frac{1}{20}$	$13\frac{11}{20}$	$1\frac{4}{10}$	$1\frac{1}{50}$

28. How many people immigrated from Europe? _____

29. How many people immigrated from Asia and South America combined? _____

30. What was the total number of immigrants? _____

31. A cake recipe calls for $2\frac{1}{3}$ cups of milk plus enough water to make $3\frac{1}{4}$ cups of liquid. How much water is used in the recipe? _____

Name _____

Subtracting Mixed Numbers

Subtract. Write the answer as a whole or mixed number in lowest terms.

1. $5\frac{2}{7} - 4\frac{2}{3}$

2. $15\frac{7}{10} - 12\frac{2}{5}$

3. $7\frac{1}{3} - 4\frac{1}{18}$

4. $2\frac{3}{8} - 2\frac{5}{16}$

_____

_____

_____

_____

5. $8\frac{5}{8} - 4\frac{7}{24}$

6. $10\frac{1}{3} - 4\frac{5}{6}$

7. $9\frac{2}{3} - 1\frac{1}{10}$

8. $12\frac{3}{11} - 8\frac{5}{11}$

_____

_____

_____

_____

9. $5\frac{1}{6} - 2\frac{5}{6}$

10. $9\frac{4}{5} - 7\frac{2}{5}$

11. $6 - 1\frac{2}{19}$

12. $3\frac{2}{3} - 1\frac{8}{15}$

_____

_____

_____

_____

13. $10\frac{4}{5} - 1\frac{14}{25}$

14. $8\frac{4}{7} - 1\frac{1}{2}$

15. $2\frac{1}{2} - 1\frac{19}{21}$

16. $12\frac{3}{4} - 5\frac{1}{7}$

_____

_____

_____

_____

17. $7\frac{4}{5} - 2\frac{5}{8}$

18. $10\frac{17}{21} - 1\frac{5}{7}$

19. $10\frac{7}{18} - 4\frac{1}{3}$

20. $15\frac{11}{14} - 14\frac{1}{7}$

_____

_____

_____

_____

21. $3\frac{5}{8} - 1\frac{9}{10}$

22. $7\frac{5}{6} - 6\frac{5}{7}$

23. $5\frac{1}{9} - 1\frac{4}{9}$

24. $8\frac{4}{5} - 3\frac{13}{20}$

_____

_____

_____

_____

Use the circle graph for Exercises 25–27.

25. What fraction of U.S. public schools are elementary schools? _____

26. What fraction of U.S. schools are colleges, universities, or in the "other" category? _____

27. What fraction of U.S. schools are secondary schools? _____

28. Jessie baked $6\frac{1}{2}$ dozen cookies for a bake sale, and $4\frac{2}{3}$ dozen of the cookies were sold. How many dozen cookies were left over?

_____

U.S. Public Schools

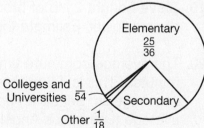

Elementary $\frac{25}{36}$

Colleges and Universities $\frac{1}{54}$

Secondary

Other $\frac{1}{18}$

Section 6B Review

Simplify. Write each answer in lowest terms.

1. $6 - 1\frac{3}{14}$ **2.** $3\frac{1}{6} - 1\frac{7}{9}$ **3.** $3 + 5\frac{7}{16}$ **4.** $10\frac{1}{4} + 17\frac{1}{4}$

_____   _____   _____   _____

5. $7 + 4\frac{2}{5}$ **6.** $8\frac{5}{17} + 1\frac{2}{17}$ **7.** $23\frac{3}{5} - 13\frac{2}{7}$ **8.** $10 - 7\frac{13}{16}$

_____   _____   _____   _____

9. $12\frac{3}{7} + 3\frac{2}{3}$ **10.** $9\frac{1}{2} - 6\frac{4}{9}$ **11.** $2\frac{2}{3} + 5\frac{1}{12}$ **12.** $3\frac{1}{5} + 1\frac{7}{8}$

_____   _____   _____   _____

13. $2\frac{1}{9} + 10$ **14.** $2\frac{4}{5} + 4\frac{4}{7}$ **15.** $6\frac{11}{20} - 4\frac{9}{10}$ **16.** $20\frac{5}{6} + 6\frac{2}{7}$

_____   _____   _____   _____

17. At Paul's Pet Palace, $\frac{3}{16}$ of the animals are dogs and $\frac{5}{24}$ of the animals are cats. What fraction of the animals are neither dogs nor cats? _____

18. At a school music festival, Judy played saxophone for $2\frac{2}{3}$ hours, Carol sang for $1\frac{3}{4}$ hours, Bob played saxophone for $1\frac{1}{4}$ hours, and Ross sang for $2\frac{3}{8}$ hours.

     a. Who had more time, the saxophone players or the singers? _____

     b. How much more? _____

19. Steve bought $2\frac{3}{4}$ lb of broccoli, $1\frac{1}{3}$ lb of carrots, and $\frac{7}{8}$ lb of cauliflower. Estimate the total amount of vegetables. _____

20. The average commute time for workers in New York is 30.6 minutes. This is 4.2 minutes longer than the average time in Los Angeles. Set up an equation and solve to find the average time in Los Angeles. *[Lesson 3-12]*

_____

21. A typical drink coaster is about 0.045 inches thick. Write this amount as a fraction in lowest terms. *[Lesson 5-7]* _____

Cumulative Review Chapters 1–6

Evaluate each expression. *[Lesson 2-8]*

1. $7 - 12 \div 3$ _____   **2.** $7 \times 4 + 8$ _____   **3.** $16 \div 2 \times 4$ _____

4. $5 \times (3 - 1)$ _____   **5.** $18 - (5 - 2)$ _____   **6.** $(7 - 4)^2$ _____

7. $6 + 4 \times 5$ _____   **8.** $10 - 2^2$ _____   **9.** $21 \div 3 + 4$ _____

10. $8 - 2 \times 3$ _____   **11.** $(7 + 2) \times 5$ _____   **12.** $2 \times (6 - 1)^2$ _____

Write each number in scientific notation. *[Lesson 3-4]*

13. 38,600   **14.** 1,420   **15.** 3,800,000   **16.** 41,500,000

_____   _____   _____   _____

17. 6,700,000,000   **18.** 17 million   **19.** 128 thousand   **20.** 7 billion

_____   _____   _____   _____

Find the perimeter. *[Lesson 4-1]*

21. _____   **22.** _____   **23.** _____   **24.** _____

7 ft
7 ft

16 cm
9 cm
18 cm

4.2 m
7.4 m

14 in.
26 in.
9 in.
32 in.

Find the LCM of each pair. *[Lesson 5-3]*

25. 5, 12 _____   **26.** 40, 30 _____   **27.** 8, 7 _____   **28.** 18, 30 _____

29. 10, 8 _____   **30.** 6, 3 _____   **31.** 18, 21 _____   **32.** 36, 18 _____

Simplify. *[Lesson 6-2]*

33. $\dfrac{2}{3} + \dfrac{1}{8}$ _____   **34.** $\dfrac{1}{6} + \dfrac{1}{5}$ _____   **35.** $\dfrac{4}{5} - \dfrac{4}{7}$ _____

36. $\dfrac{7}{13} + \dfrac{1}{3}$ _____   **37.** $\dfrac{5}{8} + \dfrac{1}{12}$ _____   **38.** $\dfrac{2}{3} - \dfrac{1}{5}$ _____

39. $\dfrac{13}{20} + \dfrac{1}{10}$ _____   **40.** $\dfrac{7}{9} - \dfrac{5}{7}$ _____   **41.** $\dfrac{1}{2} - \dfrac{1}{16}$ _____

Estimation: Products and Quotients of Fractions

Estimate.

1. $6\frac{1}{3} \times 12\frac{1}{7}$ _____

2. $7\frac{9}{10} \div 3\frac{1}{3}$ _____

3. $4\frac{2}{3} \times 3\frac{3}{4}$ _____

4. $7\frac{2}{5} \div 2\frac{2}{3}$ _____

5. $3\frac{1}{3} \times 5\frac{1}{7}$ _____

6. $12\frac{3}{5} \div 7\frac{1}{5}$ _____

7. $7\frac{5}{8} \times 9\frac{3}{5}$ _____

8. $8\frac{2}{9} \div 3\frac{3}{5}$ _____

9. $7\frac{1}{4} \times 13\frac{4}{5}$ _____

10. $9\frac{1}{4} \div 3\frac{3}{4}$ _____

11. $2\frac{1}{2} \times 3\frac{4}{9}$ _____

12. $8\frac{7}{8} \div 3\frac{2}{9}$ _____

13. $4\frac{4}{5} \times 5\frac{1}{2}$ _____

14. $8\frac{2}{3} \div 4\frac{1}{3}$ _____

15. $7\frac{2}{5} \times 7\frac{1}{2}$ _____

16. $6\frac{1}{7} \div 2\frac{2}{5}$ _____

17. $9\frac{3}{4} \times 13\frac{5}{6}$ _____

18. $10\frac{1}{9} \div 5\frac{1}{6}$ _____

19. $11\frac{5}{7} \times 4\frac{2}{3}$ _____

20. $8\frac{3}{7} \div 4\frac{1}{6}$ _____

21. $7\frac{2}{3} \times 6\frac{1}{3}$ _____

22. $11\frac{2}{3} \div 6\frac{3}{7}$ _____

23. $3\frac{7}{10} \times 11\frac{1}{8}$ _____

24. $12\frac{4}{5} \div 6\frac{1}{2}$ _____

25. $8\frac{2}{3} \times 9\frac{8}{9}$ _____

26. $10\frac{3}{8} \div 5\frac{2}{5}$ _____

27. $4\frac{2}{5} \times 6\frac{1}{2}$ _____

28. $10\frac{4}{9} \div 5\frac{5}{6}$ _____

29. $11\frac{3}{4} \times 10\frac{5}{7}$ _____

30. $10\frac{1}{6} \div 6\frac{1}{3}$ _____

31. $3\frac{2}{3} \times 10\frac{2}{5}$ _____

32. $11\frac{1}{8} \div 6\frac{1}{4}$ _____

33. $12\frac{1}{3} \times 7\frac{1}{2}$ _____

34. $8\frac{3}{5} \div 4\frac{1}{10}$ _____

35. $3\frac{3}{4} \times 3\frac{7}{10}$ _____

36. $13\frac{3}{4} \div 7\frac{1}{2}$ _____

37. $9\frac{4}{7} \times 12\frac{5}{7}$ _____

38. $9\frac{2}{5} \div 4\frac{1}{3}$ _____

39. $8\frac{7}{9} \times 9\frac{4}{9}$ _____

40. A CD box measures $5\frac{5}{8}$ inches across. A music store manager wants to display 7 CDs side-by-side on a 42-inch shelf. Is there enough room for the display?

_____

41. Computer sales to dealers increased from about $\$2\frac{2}{5}$ billion in 1984 to about $\$8\frac{1}{2}$ billion in 1995. About how many times larger was the dollar amount of sales in 1995?

_____

Multiplying by a Whole Number

Simplify.

1. $5\frac{1}{2} \times 3$ _____

2. $3 \times 4\frac{5}{6}$ _____

3. $4 \times 5\frac{2}{3}$ _____

4. $10 \times 3\frac{5}{6}$ _____

5. $12\frac{4}{7} \times 4$ _____

6. $10 \times 2\frac{1}{3}$ _____

7. $6 \times 6\frac{1}{7}$ _____

8. $4\frac{1}{2} \times 2$ _____

9. $3\frac{4}{7} \times 8$ _____

10. $12 \times 3\frac{1}{4}$ _____

11. $5 \times 5\frac{1}{3}$ _____

12. $14 \times 3\frac{1}{2}$ _____

13. $3\frac{3}{4} \times 2$ _____

14. $4 \times 9\frac{5}{9}$ _____

15. $3 \times 6\frac{2}{3}$ _____

16. $8 \times 5\frac{3}{5}$ _____

17. $10 \times 4\frac{1}{2}$ _____

18. $4 \times 12\frac{2}{3}$ _____

19. $8\frac{1}{6} \times 4$ _____

20. $11 \times 4\frac{1}{3}$ _____

21. $10\frac{1}{2} \times 5$ _____

22. $14 \times 3\frac{1}{5}$ _____

23. $2\frac{1}{2} \times 5$ _____

24. $7 \times 7\frac{5}{9}$ _____

25. $10\frac{1}{2} \times 2$ _____

26. $7\frac{1}{5} \times 6$ _____

27. $13 \times 2\frac{1}{2}$ _____

28. $6\frac{5}{6} \times 4$ _____

29. $4\frac{1}{5} \times 4$ _____

30. $12\frac{5}{7} \times 4$ _____

31. $4 \times 10\frac{1}{2}$ _____

32. $11\frac{7}{10} \times 4$ _____

33. $2 \times 13\frac{1}{4}$ _____

34. $12 \times 2\frac{4}{7}$ _____

35. $4 \times 11\frac{2}{3}$ _____

36. $8\frac{1}{7} \times 4$ _____

37. $4 \times 12\frac{1}{2}$ _____

38. $10\frac{3}{4} \times 4$ _____

39. $3 \times 12\frac{1}{5}$ _____

40. Health Complete the table for calories in a certain brand of granola cereal.

Servings	$\frac{1}{2}$	$\frac{2}{3}$	$\frac{3}{4}$	1	$1\frac{1}{3}$	$2\frac{1}{2}$
Ounces				2		
Calories				240		

41. Science The longest recorded jump by a kangaroo covered a distance of 45 feet. This is $3\frac{3}{4}$ times the longest jump from a standing position by a human. Find the length of the longest jump from a standing position by a human.

_____

Multiplying by a Fraction

Find each product.

1. $5\frac{1}{2} \times \frac{1}{2}$ _____

2. $\frac{2}{3} \times \frac{9}{10}$ _____

3. $\frac{1}{4} \times \frac{3}{5}$ _____

4. $8\frac{1}{4} \times \frac{1}{2}$ _____

5. $\frac{5}{6} \times \frac{2}{3}$ _____

6. $\frac{5}{8} \times \frac{1}{9}$ _____

7. $\frac{1}{7} \times \frac{1}{2}$ _____

8. $\frac{2}{3} \times \frac{4}{9}$ _____

9. $\frac{5}{8} \times \frac{3}{8}$ _____

10. $\frac{1}{2} \times \frac{4}{13}$ _____

11. $\frac{1}{3} \times \frac{2}{7}$ _____

12. $\frac{13}{15} \times \frac{1}{4}$ _____

13. $\frac{2}{5} \times \frac{4}{5}$ _____

14. $\frac{1}{11} \times \frac{2}{5}$ _____

15. $\frac{7}{9} \times \frac{2}{11}$ _____

16. $\frac{3}{4} \times \frac{1}{2}$ _____

17. $\frac{1}{2} \times \frac{14}{15}$ _____

18. $\frac{1}{5} \times \frac{1}{3}$ _____

19. $\frac{11}{15} \times \frac{1}{10}$ _____

20. $\frac{8}{9} \times \frac{2}{7}$ _____

21. $\frac{7}{8} \times \frac{11}{14}$ _____

22. $\frac{1}{2} \times \frac{5}{7}$ _____

23. $\frac{3}{4} \times \frac{1}{3}$ _____

24. $\frac{1}{2} \times \frac{7}{8}$ _____

25. $\frac{2}{15} \times \frac{1}{2}$ _____

26. $\frac{1}{3} \times \frac{4}{5}$ _____

27. $\frac{10}{11} \times 5\frac{2}{3}$ _____

28. $\frac{10}{11} \times \frac{5}{6}$ _____

29. $\frac{1}{5} \times \frac{1}{2}$ _____

30. $\frac{3}{10} \times 2\frac{1}{2}$ _____

31. $\frac{12}{13} \times \frac{3}{10}$ _____

32. $\frac{2}{3} \times \frac{1}{3}$ _____

33. $\frac{2}{3} \times \frac{7}{9}$ _____

34. $\frac{5}{12} \times 3\frac{7}{12}$ _____

35. $\frac{1}{6} \times \frac{2}{7}$ _____

36. $\frac{3}{5} \times \frac{7}{11}$ _____

37. $\frac{1}{2} \times 7\frac{9}{13}$ _____

38. $\frac{2}{3} \times \frac{2}{5}$ _____

39. $\frac{2}{7} \times \frac{1}{10}$ _____

40. **Science** The total weight of all of the insects in the world is about $\frac{7}{20}$ of a billion tons. The total weight of all humans is about $\frac{1}{3}$ of this amount. Find the total weight of all humans. _____

41. A recipe for minestrone soup calls for $3\frac{1}{2}$ cups of vegetable stock. How much stock would you use to make $\frac{2}{3}$ of the amount of soup in the original recipe? _____

Section 7A Review

Estimate each product or quotient.

1. $4\frac{5}{6} \times 12\frac{2}{5}$ _____

2. $7\frac{3}{4} \div 2\frac{2}{3}$ _____

3. $3\frac{4}{9} \times 10\frac{2}{7}$ _____

4. $9\frac{1}{4} \div 4\frac{4}{7}$ _____

5. $11\frac{1}{2} \times 13\frac{2}{5}$ _____

6. $8\frac{4}{7} \div 3\frac{5}{9}$ _____

Simplify.

7. $4\frac{1}{9} \times 4$ _____

8. $8 \times 3\frac{1}{2}$ _____

9. $1\frac{1}{3} \times 2\frac{1}{2}$ _____

10. $4\frac{1}{10} \times 8$ _____

11. $\frac{1}{2} \times 4$ _____

12. $5 \times 2\frac{3}{8}$ _____

13. The table shows the ingredients in a recipe for papaya ice cream from *Kathy Cooks Naturally*. Complete the table to show how much of each ingredient you would use to make 4 times or 6 times the amount of the original recipe.

Ingredient	Ripe papaya	Orange juice	Lemon juice	Whipping cream	Honey
Original recipe	$1\frac{1}{2}$ cups	$\frac{1}{2}$ cup	$\frac{3}{16}$ cup	$1\frac{1}{2}$ cups	$\frac{1}{2}$ cup
4 times					
6 times					

14. Fancy tomatoes are selling for $1.95 per pound. Can you buy $2\frac{1}{4}$ pounds if you only have $4.00? _____

15. Mrs. Gonzales bought $3\frac{1}{8}$ pounds of candy for Halloween. She gave away $\frac{3}{5}$ of the candy. How much candy was left over? _____

16. **Fine Arts** Rodney is making a macramé belt that is to be $1\frac{1}{4}$ meters long. If $\frac{1}{3}$ of the belt has been completed, how many meters of the belt have been completed? _____

17. Some giant dump trucks use tires with a diameter of 12.5 feet. Find the area of a wheel with this tire. *[Lesson 4-8]* _____

18. Rick had $\frac{7}{8}$ of a cup of lemon juice. After making a pie, he had $\frac{1}{2}$ cup of lemon juice left. How much lemon juice did he use in the pie? *[Lesson 6-3]* _____

Dividing Whole Numbers
by Fractions

Simplify.

1. $11 \div \frac{1}{7}$ _____

2. $6 \div \frac{1}{3}$ _____

3. $3 \div 1\frac{5}{8}$ _____

4. $7 \div \frac{2}{3}$ _____

5. $4 \div \frac{3}{4}$ _____

6. $11 \div \frac{3}{4}$ _____

7. $12 \div \frac{2}{5}$ _____

8. $11 \div \frac{4}{9}$ _____

9. $12 \div 3\frac{1}{2}$ _____

10. $7 \div \frac{3}{10}$ _____

11. $11 \div \frac{1}{2}$ _____

12. $3 \div \frac{2}{5}$ _____

13. $5 \div 2\frac{2}{9}$ _____

14. $7 \div 2\frac{8}{9}$ _____

15. $8 \div \frac{1}{3}$ _____

16. $8 \div 1\frac{1}{4}$ _____

17. $8 \div 1\frac{5}{6}$ _____

18. $10 \div 1\frac{7}{9}$ _____

19. $7 \div 1\frac{1}{5}$ _____

20. $4 \div 4\frac{1}{3}$ _____

21. $3 \div 4\frac{1}{5}$ _____

22. $10 \div 1\frac{1}{2}$ _____

23. $6 \div \frac{1}{2}$ _____

24. $7 \div \frac{2}{9}$ _____

25. $3 \div 2\frac{3}{5}$ _____

26. $11 \div 1\frac{3}{10}$ _____

27. $10 \div 1\frac{5}{9}$ _____

28. $7 \div 2\frac{4}{7}$ _____

29. $8 \div 1\frac{1}{3}$ _____

30. $8 \div 1\frac{1}{2}$ _____

31. $12 \div 1\frac{1}{3}$ _____

32. $8 \div \frac{3}{7}$ _____

33. $5 \div 2\frac{2}{5}$ _____

34. $8 \div \frac{1}{7}$ _____

35. $8 \div 2\frac{1}{3}$ _____

36. $5 \div \frac{2}{3}$ _____

37. $7 \div 2\frac{5}{9}$ _____

38. $3 \div \frac{1}{3}$ _____

39. $11 \div 2\frac{2}{3}$ _____

40. $3 \div 2\frac{1}{3}$ _____

41. $5 \div 1\frac{1}{5}$ _____

42. $4 \div \frac{2}{5}$ _____

43. Science A baby walrus is 4 feet long. This is $\frac{2}{5}$ of the length of
an adult male. What is the length of an adult male walrus? _____

44. Measurement One yard (36 inches) is equal to $\frac{2}{11}$ of a rod.
How many inches are in a rod? _____

Dividing Fractions by Fractions

Simplify.

1. $1\frac{4}{5} \div \frac{1}{3}$ _____

2. $1\frac{2}{3} \div \frac{1}{8}$ _____

3. $3\frac{4}{7} \div 3\frac{1}{2}$ _____

4. $3\frac{4}{5} \div 1\frac{5}{7}$ _____

5. $\frac{2}{5} \div 4\frac{3}{5}$ _____

6. $4\frac{1}{8} \div \frac{3}{7}$ _____

7. $\frac{1}{2} \div \frac{2}{5}$ _____

8. $2\frac{4}{5} \div 4\frac{3}{4}$ _____

9. $\frac{5}{6} \div 1\frac{3}{4}$ _____

10. $1\frac{5}{7} \div 1\frac{2}{3}$ _____

11. $\frac{8}{9} \div \frac{1}{2}$ _____

12. $\frac{1}{4} \div \frac{2}{5}$ _____

13. $\frac{1}{3} \div 2\frac{1}{6}$ _____

14. $1\frac{4}{9} \div \frac{6}{7}$ _____

15. $1\frac{3}{4} \div \frac{4}{5}$ _____

16. $\frac{1}{3} \div \frac{2}{5}$ _____

17. $1\frac{1}{3} \div 1\frac{3}{4}$ _____

18. $\frac{1}{3} \div \frac{2}{7}$ _____

19. $\frac{1}{2} \div 3\frac{1}{4}$ _____

20. $2\frac{1}{4} \div 3\frac{4}{9}$ _____

21. $4\frac{2}{7} \div 1\frac{1}{6}$ _____

22. $\frac{4}{5} \div 3\frac{2}{5}$ _____

23. $1\frac{1}{5} \div \frac{1}{3}$ _____

24. $\frac{4}{5} \div \frac{1}{6}$ _____

25. $\frac{8}{9} \div 2\frac{5}{7}$ _____

26. $1\frac{1}{4} \div 2\frac{2}{3}$ _____

27. $\frac{1}{4} \div 1\frac{5}{9}$ _____

28. $\frac{1}{4} \div \frac{1}{4}$ _____

29. $1\frac{7}{8} \div 1\frac{1}{4}$ _____

30. $1\frac{3}{4} \div \frac{1}{5}$ _____

31. $4\frac{2}{7} \div 1\frac{1}{2}$ _____

32. $5\frac{1}{7} \div 2\frac{1}{2}$ _____

33. $1\frac{1}{9} \div \frac{1}{5}$ _____

34. $1\frac{1}{2} \div 1\frac{2}{3}$ _____

35. $\frac{7}{8} \div \frac{2}{7}$ _____

36. $1\frac{5}{8} \div \frac{5}{9}$ _____

37. $\frac{1}{4} \div \frac{4}{5}$ _____

38. $1\frac{1}{2} \div 3\frac{1}{2}$ _____

39. $1\frac{3}{5} \div \frac{1}{3}$ _____

40. $\frac{1}{2} \div 3\frac{5}{7}$ _____

41. $1\frac{1}{3} \div 1\frac{2}{3}$ _____

42. $1\frac{1}{2} \div 2\frac{3}{4}$ _____

43. Measurement A cake recipe calls for $\frac{5}{8}$ of a cup of butter. One tablespoon equals $\frac{1}{16}$ of a cup. How many tablespoons of butter are used to make the cake?

_____

44. Geography One square mile equals $\frac{1}{36}$ of a township. The area of Austin, Texas, is $6\frac{4}{9}$ townships. Find the area in square miles.

_____

Solving Fraction Equations: Multiplication and Division

Solve.

1. $n \div 4\frac{1}{3} = \frac{1}{2}$

$n =$ _____

2. $2\frac{6}{7}f = \frac{1}{3}$

$f =$ _____

3. $f \div 2\frac{5}{7} = \frac{1}{2}$

$f =$ _____

4. $n \div 3\frac{3}{5} = 2\frac{1}{3}$

$n =$ _____

5. $n \div 1\frac{3}{5} = 1$

$n =$ _____

6. $\frac{1}{2}u = 5\frac{3}{5}$

$u =$ _____

7. $q \div 2\frac{1}{3} = \frac{3}{8}$

$q =$ _____

8. $c \div 2\frac{4}{5} = \frac{1}{2}$

$c =$ _____

9. $b \div \frac{2}{3} = 2\frac{6}{7}$

$b =$ _____

10. $\frac{1}{4}n = 2$

$n =$ _____

11. $t \div 1\frac{1}{7} = 3$

$t =$ _____

12. $h \div 2\frac{2}{5} = \frac{3}{5}$

$h =$ _____

13. $2f = \frac{1}{4}$

$f =$ _____

14. $2z = 3\frac{2}{3}$

$z =$ _____

15. $2\frac{1}{4}v = \frac{1}{4}$

$v =$ _____

16. $h \div 3\frac{1}{8} = 2$

$h =$ _____

17. $v \div \frac{1}{3} = \frac{2}{5}$

$v =$ _____

18. $3\frac{7}{10}q = 1$

$q =$ _____

19. $h \div \frac{7}{10} = \frac{1}{2}$

$h =$ _____

20. $1c = 1\frac{1}{3}$

$c =$ _____

21. $w \div 1\frac{1}{2} = 3\frac{1}{4}$

$w =$ _____

22. $d \div 2\frac{1}{8} = 2\frac{1}{3}$

$d =$ _____

23. $v \div \frac{2}{3} = 1\frac{1}{2}$

$v =$ _____

24. $z \div \frac{1}{3} = 1$

$z =$ _____

25. $t \div 2 = 2$

$t =$ _____

26. $b \div 1 = 1\frac{2}{5}$

$b =$ _____

27. $\frac{5}{9}z = \frac{1}{3}$

$z =$ _____

28. $1\frac{7}{10}m = 4$

$m =$ _____

29. The largest U.S. standard postage stamp ever issued has a width of $1\frac{1}{11}$ inches, which was $\frac{3}{4}$ of the height of the stamp. Write and solve an equation to find the height of the stamp.

_____

30. Candace said, "I'm thinking of a fraction. If I divide it by $2\frac{1}{2}$, I get $\frac{3}{11}$." What fraction was Candace thinking of? _____

Section 7B Review

Simplify.

1. $1\frac{7}{8} \div 1\frac{5}{7}$ _____

2. $7 \div 3\frac{3}{5}$ _____

3. $1\frac{5}{6} \times 5\frac{2}{3}$ _____

4. $3 \div 2\frac{1}{2}$ _____

5. $3\frac{1}{3} \times 7\frac{1}{2}$ _____

6. $3\frac{3}{5} \div \frac{1}{3}$ _____

7. $2\frac{1}{2} \div 7\frac{2}{3}$ _____

8. $2\frac{3}{5} \times 8$ _____

9. Measurement One teaspoon is $\frac{1}{3}$ of a tablespoon. A bread recipe calls for 2 tablespoons of yeast. How many teaspoons is this? _____

10. Measurement There are $1\frac{3}{25}$ American tons in one British ton (long ton). How many British tons are in 7 American tons? _____

Solve.

11. $1\frac{2}{7}g = \frac{1}{2}$

12. $x \div \frac{1}{2} = 1\frac{1}{3}$

13. $\frac{7}{8}f = \frac{3}{5}$

14. $s \div 3 = \frac{3}{4}$

$g =$ _____

$x =$ _____

$f =$ _____

$s =$ _____

15. Write and solve an equation to find the number of furlongs in 12 rods. (1 rod = $\frac{1}{40}$ furlong)

_____

16. Write and solve an equation to find the number of pounds in 8 kilograms. (1 kilogram $\approx 2\frac{1}{5}$ pounds)

_____

17. The road distance from Toledo, Ohio, to Detroit, Michigan, is 4720 chains. One mile = 80 chains. Explain how you could use either multiplication or division to find the number of miles from Toledo to Detroit.

_____

18. Science The largest birds' egg ever measured was laid by an ostrich in 1988 and had a mass of 2.32 kilograms. A typical albatross egg has about one fourth of this mass. Find the mass of an albatross egg. *[Lesson 3-12]* _____

19. Fine Arts Rodin's bronze sculpture of Jules Dalov is $20\frac{3}{4}$ inches tall. His marble *Hand of God* is $15\frac{7}{8}$ inches taller. Find the height of the *Hand of God*. _____

Name _____

Cumulative Review Chapters 1–7

Write the phrase as an expression. *[Lesson 2-11]*

1. y divided by 7 _____

2. m times 5 _____

3. 15 less than u _____

4. one-third of k _____

5. d increased by 12 _____

6. c doubled _____

7. half of g _____

8. p cubed _____

Multiply. *[Lesson 3-9]*

9. 0.01×6.45 _____

10. 895×0.001 _____

11. 2.83×9.7 _____

12. 0.38×0.08 _____

13. 12.7×0.85 _____

14. 2.3×18 _____

15. 0.43×0.7 _____

16. 8.41×0.03 _____

17. 34.8×1.2 _____

Convert. *[Lesson 4-2]*

18. 85 g = _____ kg

19. 42 kg = _____ g

20. 3.82 mL = _____ L

21. 73 cm = _____ m

22. 6.2 L = _____ mL

23. 9.4 m = _____ mm

24. 183 m = _____ km

25. 31 mm = _____ m

26. 2.9 km = _____ cm

Simplify. *[Lessons 7-2 to 7-5]*

27. $\frac{1}{3} \div 4\frac{1}{2}$ _____

28. $3 \div 1\frac{3}{4}$ _____

29. $2 \div 10\frac{1}{2}$ _____

30. $4\frac{1}{2} \div 15$ _____

31. $2 \div 3\frac{3}{4}$ _____

32. $2\frac{2}{5} \times 6$ _____

33. $4\frac{3}{4} \div 1\frac{1}{5}$ _____

34. $6\frac{1}{2} \times 7\frac{1}{2}$ _____

Solve. *[Lesson 7-6]*

35. $\frac{1}{9}q = \frac{1}{6}$

36. $k \div \frac{1}{6} = \frac{7}{9}$

37. $g \div 1\frac{3}{4} = 4$

38. $p \div 2\frac{1}{2} = 2\frac{1}{4}$

$q =$ _____

$k =$ _____

$g =$ _____

$p =$ _____

39. $p \div \frac{1}{4} = \frac{7}{9}$

40. $\frac{1}{4}n = 2\frac{2}{3}$

41. $v \div \frac{1}{5} = 3$

42. $f \div \frac{5}{9} = 2\frac{1}{2}$

$p =$ _____

$n =$ _____

$v =$ _____

$f =$ _____

Classifying Lines

Draw an example of each.

1. $\overline{GH}$

2. $\overrightarrow{GH}$

3. $\overleftrightarrow{GH}$

4. $\overrightarrow{PQ}$

5. $\overleftrightarrow{PQ}$

6. $\overline{PQ}$

Describe the relationship between the lines, rays, or segments.

7. _____

8. _____

9. _____

10. _____

Tell whether each statement is always, sometimes, or never true.

11. Perpendicular lines intersect.

_____

12. Rays that are not parallel intersect.

_____

13. The blue lines on a sheet of standard notebook paper are perpendicular.

_____

14. The diagram shows a simplified drawing of a truck.

  a. Name two pairs of parallel line segments.

  _____

  b. Name two pairs of perpendicular line segments.

  _____

  c. Name two line segments that intersect but are not perpendicular.

  _____

Classifying Angles

Classify each angle as acute, right, obtuse, or straight.

1. _____

2. _____

3. _____

4. _____

5. _____

6. _____

7. _____

8. _____
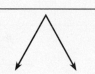

Name each angle three ways.

9. _____

10. _____

11. _____

Tell whether each statement is always, sometimes, or never true.

12. The sides of a straight angle lie on the same line. _____

13. The sides of an acute angle are parallel. _____

14. The sides of a right angle are perpendicular. _____

Measurement Classify the angle made by the hands of a clock at each time.

15. 2:00 _____

16. 5:00 _____

17. 7:45 _____

18. 9:00 _____

19. 10:15 _____

20. 4:40 _____

21. Use the figure at the right. Name two angles of each type.

Acute: _____

Right: _____

Obtuse: _____

Straight: _____

Name _____

Measuring Angles

Estimate the measure of each angle. Then measure each with a protractor.

1. _____ **2.** _____ **3.** _____ **4.** _____

Draw an angle of each measure. Then classify each as acute, obtuse, or right.

5. 60° _____ **6.** 105° _____ **7.** 90° _____ **8.** 15° _____

State the angle measure that is complementary to the given angle.

9. 18° _____ **10.** 88° _____ **11.** 32° _____ **12.** 60° _____

13. 41° _____ **14.** 26° _____ **15.** 7° _____ **16.** 78° _____

State the angle measure that is supplementary to the given angle.

17. 85° _____ **18.** 100° _____ **19.** 23° _____ **20.** 163° _____

21. 135° _____ **22.** 36° _____ **23.** 120° _____ **24.** 71° _____

Read each statement and tell if it is always, sometimes, or never true.

25. An obtuse angle and an acute angle are complementary. _____

26. A pair of supplementary angles includes an obtuse
angle and an acute angle.   _____

27. Name a pair of complementary angles and a pair
of supplementary angles in the figure.

Complementary: _____

Supplementary: _____

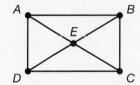

Name _____

Section 8A Review

Describe the relationship between the lines, rays, or segments.

1. _____

2. _____

3. _____

4. _____

Classify each angle as acute, right, obtuse, or straight.

5. _____ **6.** _____ **7.** _____ **8.** _____

Measure each angle and find its complement and supplement.

9. measure: _____

complement: _____

supplement: _____

10. measure: _____

complement: _____

supplement: _____

11. measure: _____

complement: _____

supplement: _____

12. Science The gar is an armored fish that has survived since the age of dinosaurs. It is 150 centimeters long. How many meters is this? *[Lesson 4-2]*

_____

13. During the 1896 Olympic Games, Thomas Burke completed the 400-meter dash in $54\frac{1}{5}$ seconds. In 1992, Quincy Watts beat this time by $10\frac{7}{10}$ seconds. What was Watts' time? *[Lesson 6-6]*

_____

Exploring Angles in a Triangle

For Exercises 1–8, classify each triangle as acute, right, or obtuse.

1. _____ 2. _____ 3. _____ 4. _____

5. $m\angle T = 47°$, $m\angle U = 87°$, $m\angle V = 46°$ **6.** $m\angle D = 73°$, $m\angle E = 90°$, $m\angle F = 17°$

_____   _____

7. $m\angle G = 51°$, $m\angle P = 68°$, $m\angle Z = 61°$ **8.** $m\angle A = 67°$, $m\angle R = 13°$, $m\angle F = 100°$

_____   _____

Use a protractor to determine the measures of all angles in each triangle.

9. _____ 10. _____ 11. _____ 12. _____

Find the measure of the missing angle in each triangle.

13. $m\angle G = 94°$, $m\angle H = 47°$,   **14.** $m\angle K = 81°$, $m\angle L = 53°$,

   $m\angle I =$ _____ $m\angle M =$ _____

15. $m\angle P = 38°$, $m\angle Q = 45°$,   **16.** $m\angle B = 30°$, $m\angle S = 60°$,

   $m\angle R =$ _____ $m\angle U =$ _____

For Exercises 17–20, decide whether the angle measurements can
form a triangle. If a triangle can be formed, draw and classify it.

17. 35°, 65°, 90°   **18.** 70°, 55°, 55°

_____   _____

19. 30°, 40°, 110°   **20.** 45°, 55°, 65°

_____   _____

Exploring Sides of a Triangle

For Exercises 1–8, classify each triangle as scalene, equilateral, or isosceles.

1. _____

2. _____

3. _____

4. _____

5. Sides: 8 cm, 9 cm, 11 cm

_____

6. Sides: 12 yd, 15 yd, 12 yd

_____

7. Sides: 21 km, 21 km, 21 km

_____

8. Sides: 9 ft, 13 ft, 14 ft

_____

State whether the given lengths can form a triangle.
If they can, draw the triangle and classify it.

9. 9 in., 3 in., 10 in.

_____

10. 20 cm, 15 cm, 5 cm

_____

11. 8 ft, 8 ft, 8 ft

_____

12. 8 m, 8 m, 12 m

_____

13. Carolyn made a triangular painting and measured its sides.
The numbers she wrote down were 35 cm, 55 cm, and 95 cm.
She said, "That can't be right. I must have made a mistake."
How did she know?

_____

Name _____

Polygons

Name each polygon and tell if it is regular or irregular.

1. _____ 2. _____

3. _____ 4. _____

Draw an example of each figure and classify each of the angles in your drawing.

5. Irregular hexagon   **6.** Regular quadilateral

_____   _____

_____   _____

7. Irregular triangle   **8.** Regular octagon

_____   _____

_____   _____

What kind of polygon is each mask?

9. _____ 10. _____ 11. _____ 12. _____

13. Social Science The offices of the U.S. Department of Defense
are located in an Arlington, Virginia, building called the Pentagon.
How many sides do you think the shape of this building has? _____

Name _____

Quadrilaterals

Answer true or false.

1. Some rectangles are also rhombuses.   _____

2. All quadrilaterals are either trapezoids or parallelograms.   _____

3. A square is a kind of trapezoid.   _____

Classify each figure in as many ways as possible.

4. _____   5. _____

   _____   _____

Draw an example of each figure. Classify each of the angles in your drawing.

6. A rhombus that   7. A rectangle that   8. A parallelogram that is not
   is not a square   is not a square   a rectangle or a rhombus

   _____   _____   _____

   _____   _____   _____

Measurement Given the information, can you determine the lengths
of each figure's sides? If so, give the lengths.

9. A rhombus with a perimeter of 44 inches.   _____

10. A trapezoid with three 5-meter sides   _____

11. Classify each shape in the jack-o-lantern in as many ways as possible.

   Eyes _____

   Nose _____

   Mouth _____

96

Name _____

Section 8B Review

Use the letters to name each angle in three ways.

1. _____

2. _____

3. _____

Classify each triangle by its sides. Find the measure of each missing angle.

4. _____

5. _____

6. _____

Draw an example of each figure.

7. Irregular octagon

8. Regular triangle

9. Irregular pentagon

Classify each figure in as many ways as possible.

10.

_____

_____

11.

_____

_____

12. Geography The figure at the right shows the approximate shape of Manitoba, Canada. Find the approximate area of Manitoba. *[Lesson 4-9]*

_____

13. Science A typical female swallowtail butterfly weighs about $\frac{11}{20}$ gram. Find the weight of 12 female swallowtails. *[Lesson 7-2]*

_____

Name _____

Flips and Line Symmetry

Tell if the picture has line symmetry. If it does, tell how many lines of symmetry it has.

1. _____

2. _____

3. _____

4. _____

Tell if each line is a line of symmetry.

5. _____

6. _____

7. _____

8. _____

Tell if each pair of figures are congruent. If *not,* draw a figure congruent to each.

9. _____

10. _____

11. _____

Use the design for Exercises 12 and 13.

12. Name the congruent figures in the design.

_____

13. Tell whether the design has line symmetry.
If it does, draw the line(s) of symmetry.

_____

14. Hexagonal tiles can be used to cover floors because
they fit together nicely. Draw all lines of symmetry in
the figure.

Turns and Rotational Symmetry

What is the least rotation that will land the figure on top of itself?

1. _____ 2. _____ 3. _____ 4. _____

Draw a 45° clockwise rotation of the figure.

5.

6.

7.

8.

Estimate the number of degrees and state the direction in which each
figure has been rotated.

9. _____ 10. _____

11. _____ 12. _____

13. **Fine Arts** A mirror illustrated in Jan van Eyck's
The Betrothal of the Arnolfini has the shape
shown at the right. If the mirror is rotated 360°,
how many times will it land on itself?

_____

Tessellations

Name the polygon that is tessellated in each design.

1. _____

2. _____

3. _____

4. _____

State if each figure tessellates. Make a drawing to show your answer.

5. _____

6. _____

7. _____

8. _____

9. Is each shaded polygon a translation of one of the white polygons?

_____

_____

_____

Name _____

Section 8C Review

Name each polygon and tell if it has line symmetry. If it does, tell how many lines of symmetry it has.

1. _____   **2.** _____

3. _____   **4.** _____

5. _____   **6.** _____

State if each figure will tessellate. Make a drawing to show your answer.

7. _____   **8.** _____

9. _____   **10.** _____

11. Science A running cheetah completed one stride (23 feet) in 0.28 seconds. Using the formula distance = rate × time, write and solve an equation to find this cheetah's speed in feet per second. *[Lesson 3-12]*

_____

12. A $7\frac{3}{4}$-pound tomato was grown in Oklahoma in 1986. Write and solve an equation to find the number of $\frac{3}{8}$-pound servings that could be made from this tomato. *[Lesson 7-6]*

_____

Name _____

Cumulative Review Chapters 1–8

Find the area. [Lesson 4-6]

1. _____

2. _____

3. _____

4. _____

Find the LCM of each pair. [Lesson 5-3]

5. 4, 10 _____   6. 13, 4 _____   7. 9, 6 _____   8. 8, 32 _____

9. 30, 70 _____   10. 50, 6 _____   11. 2, 15 _____   12. 42, 60 _____

13. 27, 16 _____   14. 9, 15 _____   15. 16, 30 _____   16. 36, 54 _____

Solve. [Lesson 6-3]

17. $c + \frac{3}{4} = \frac{7}{8}$ 18. $x - \frac{3}{16} = \frac{1}{2}$ 19. $p + \frac{2}{3} = \frac{11}{12}$ 20. $k - \frac{1}{16} = \frac{1}{3}$

$c =$ _____ $x =$ _____ $p =$ _____ $k =$ _____

21. $u + \frac{1}{2} = \frac{4}{7}$ 22. $t - \frac{2}{11} = \frac{2}{3}$ 23. $v + \frac{3}{5} = \frac{5}{6}$ 24. $h - \frac{1}{6} = \frac{1}{4}$

$u =$ _____ $t =$ _____ $v =$ _____ $h =$ _____

Measure each angle with a protractor. [Lesson 8-3]

25. _____   26. _____   27. _____

Classify each triangle as scalene, equilateral, or isosceles. [Lesson 8-5]

28. _____   29. _____   30. _____

Understanding Integers

Locate each integer on the number line.

1. 1

2. −3

3. −1

4. 4

Compare using > or <.

5. 7 ◯ −7   **6.** −5 ◯ −6   **7.** 0 ◯ −3   **8.** 16 ◯ −17

9. −12 ◯ 9   **10.** 4 ◯ 0   **11.** −11 ◯ −7   **12.** 14 ◯ −12

13. −6 ◯ 8   **14.** 12 ◯ −11   **15.** −8 ◯ 0   **16.** 5 ◯ −1

Order from greatest to least.

17. 17, −15, −20, 19

18. −74, −83, −62, −77

19. 5, 0, −8, 3, −6

20. −66, 78, 42, −58

Write each number as an integer.

21. Jason has $318 in his bank account.

22. The temperature is 9°F below zero.

23. Rover weighs 36 pounds.

24. Sylvia owes $520.

25. The Aslam family made $253 at their garage sale, but they had to pay $18 for advertising and signs. Write the money amounts as integers.

26. Science High and low tide levels are reported using positive and negative numbers. The tides for June 6, 1997, in Broad Creek, South Carolina, were −12, 232, −17, and 272 centimeters. Write these numbers in order from the lowest tide to the highest.

Adding Integers

State each number's opposite.

1. −2 _____   **2.** 7 _____   **3.** 14 _____   **4.** −52 _____

5. −16 _____   **6.** 11 _____   **7.** −23 _____   **8.** 36 _____

State if the sum is positive, negative, or zero.

9. −5 + 5   **10.** 9 + (−12)   **11.** −38 + 5   **12.** −3 + 17

_____   _____   _____   _____

13. 21 + (−9)   **14.** −2 + 1   **15.** 6 + (−6)   **16.** −64 + 38

_____   _____   _____   _____

17. 7 + (−3)   **18.** 17 + (−3)   **19.** −47 + 47   **20.** 43 + (−35)

_____   _____   _____   _____

Add.

21. −7 + 12 _____   **22.** 35 + (−1) _____   **23.** −10 + (−12) _____

24. −6 + (−5) _____   **25.** 0 + (−6) _____   **26.** 50 + (−2) _____

27. 1 + (−7) _____   **28.** −15 + 15 _____   **29.** 2 + (−9) _____

30. −31 + 3 _____   **31.** 4 + (−12) _____   **32.** −23 + 8 _____

33. 10 + (−15) _____   **34.** 42 + 16 _____   **35.** −1 + (−4) _____

36. −9 + (−14) _____   **37.** 12 + (−12) _____   **38.** 25 + 6 _____

39. 5 + (−65) _____   **40.** −20 + 0 _____   **41.** 3 + (−8) _____

42. −4 + 27 _____   **43.** −8 + 4 _____   **44.** 8 + 2 _____

45. Which height is higher, −83 feet or the opposite of −88 feet?

_____

46. U.S. business inventories decreased 10 billion dollars in 1991,
then increased 7 billion dollars the next year. What was the
overall change in business inventories for the two years? _____

Name _____

Subtracting Integers

Write a subtraction equation that shows the distance between *P* and *Q* on each number line.

1. _____

2. _____

3. _____

4. _____

5. _____

6. _____

Subtract.

7. $-1 - (-15)$ _____

8. $20 - 3$ _____

9. $11 - (-5)$ _____

10. $20 - 2$ _____

11. $-12 - (-12)$ _____

12. $-2 - (-4)$ _____

13. $7 - 13$ _____

14. $3 - 5$ _____

15. $-6 - 11$ _____

16. $9 - 16$ _____

17. $0 - (-7)$ _____

18. $-4 - (-1)$ _____

19. $5 - (-3)$ _____

20. $-9 - 25$ _____

21. $-18 - 10$ _____

22. $-11 - (-8)$ _____

23. $-16 - 9$ _____

24. $10 - (-9)$ _____

25. $-25 - (-40)$ _____

26. $-48 - 0$ _____

27. $-8 - 7$ _____

28. $50 - (-8)$ _____

29. $-66 - (-10)$ _____

30. $30 - (-42)$ _____

31. $12 - (-6)$ _____

32. $8 - 18$ _____

33. $15 - (-8)$ _____

34. $-5 - 1$ _____

35. $4 - (-22)$ _____

36. $-10 - 35$ _____

37. $1 - (-2)$ _____

38. $2 - 6$ _____

39. $6 - 21$ _____

40. $-3 - 17$ _____

41. $-7 - 4$ _____

42. $40 - (-12)$ _____

43. Geography The elevation of New Orleans, Louisiana, is 8 feet below sea level. The elevation of Lake Champlain, Vermont, is 95 feet above sea level. How much higher is Lake Champlain than New Orleans? _____

44. In Fairbanks, Alaska, a typical January temperature is $-13°F$ and a typical April temperature is $30°F$. What is the difference between these temperatures? _____

Multiplying and Dividing Integers

Multiply.

1. -2×4 _____ **2.** -5×6 _____ **3.** $4 \times (-5)$ _____

4. $-1 \times (-13)$ _____ **5.** $2 \times (-8)$ _____ **6.** 5×19 _____

7. $-3 \times (-6)$ _____ **8.** $7 \times (-4)$ _____ **9.** -8×11 _____

10. -6×20 _____ **11.** $-3 \times (-12)$ _____ **12.** -4×5 _____

13. -7×7 _____ **14.** $6 \times (-10)$ _____ **15.** $-8 \times (-15)$ _____

Divide.

16. $-8 \div (-4)$ _____ **17.** $-20 \div 4$ _____ **18.** $-6 \div 2$ _____

19. $-12 \div 3$ _____ **20.** $-5 \div 5$ _____ **21.** $-18 \div (-3)$ _____

22. $-45 \div (-5)$ _____ **23.** $-4 \div (-1)$ _____ **24.** $-48 \div 6$ _____

25. $-6 \div (-2)$ _____ **26.** $0 \div (-5)$ _____ **27.** $12 \div (-6)$ _____

28. $56 \div 8$ _____ **29.** $-35 \div (-7)$ _____ **30.** $48 \div (-8)$ _____

Complete each pattern.

31. $-15 \div 5 = -3$ **32.** $(-3)^1 = -3$ **33.** $-7 \times (-3) = 21$ **34.** $-12 \div (-4) = 3$

____ $\div 5 = -2$ $(-3)^2 = 9$ $-7 \times (-2) =$ __ $-8 \div (-4) =$ ____

$-5 \div$ __ $= -1$ $(-3)^3 = -27$ ___ $\times (-1) = 7$ ___ $\div (-4) = 1$

$0 \div 5 =$ ____ $(-3)^4 =$ _____ $-7 \times$ ___ $= 0$ ___ $\div (-4) = 0$

$5 \div 5 =$ ____ $(-3)^5 =$ _____   ___ $\times 1 = -7$ __ $\div (-4) =$ __

35. The average daily high temperature in Rome, Italy, typically drops 15°F over the 3 months from July to October. Assuming that it drops the same amount every month, how many degrees does it drop in one month? _____

36. Ricky is playing a game in which blue chips are worth 8 points each and red chips are worth −5 points each. Ricky has 7 blue chips and 11 red chips. Find the value of the blue chips and the red chips.

Blue _____   Red _____

Section 9A Review

Simplify.

1. −3 + 15 _____

2. 3 × (−7) _____

3. 4 − (−9) _____

4. 28 ÷ (−7) _____

5. 10 + (−4) _____

6. −10 × 4 _____

7. 15 − (−6) _____

8. −100 ÷ (−10) _____

9. −6 + (−12) _____

10. −6 × (−4) _____

11. 8 − 21 _____

12. −63 ÷ 9 _____

13. 7 + (−11) _____

14. 12 × (−3) _____

15. −7 − 5 _____

16. The CD Recyclery sells used CDs for $10 each and buys them for $6 each. Bob paid $20 when he bought and sold the same number of CDs. How many CDs did he buy? _____

For Exercises 17–20, solve each problem and state the operation you used.

17. Raymond lost $800 on the stock market each month for 5 months in a row. What was the overall change in the value of his stock account?

18. Shelly tossed a ball from the top of a cliff. The ball rose 16 feet, and then fell 40 feet to the bottom of the cliff. How tall was the cliff?

19. Taylor wrote a check for $18 on the same day his bank paid interest to his account. If his account balance changed $13 that day, how much interest did he earn?

20. A feather fell 10 feet in 5 seconds. How far did it fall in 1 second? _____

21. A recipe for bread includes $\frac{1}{4}$ cup of oil, $\frac{1}{2}$ cup of sugar, and $\frac{2}{3}$ cup of milk. Write each measurement as a decimal. *[Lesson 5-7]*

Oil _____   Sugar _____   Milk _____

22. The flag of Finland is shown. Does this flag have line symmetry? If so, draw the line or lines of symmetry. *[Lesson 8-8]*

_____

The Coordinate Plane

Give the coordinates of each point.

1. H _____

2. Q _____

3. A _____

4. L _____

5. T _____

6. C _____

7. M _____

8. X _____

9. F _____

10. N _____

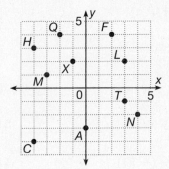

State which quadrant each point is in.

11. (3, −21) _____

12. (−15, −42) _____

13. (18, 10) _____

14. (−24, 29) _____

15. (35, 11) _____

16. (−6, 17) _____

Plot and label each point.

17. J(3, −2)

18. E(3, 2)

19. W(−1, −4)

20. R(1, 0)

21. B(−2, 2)

22. Z(2, 3)

23. P(−4, 1)

24. G(−3, −1)

25. Y(0, −3)

26. S(2, −4)

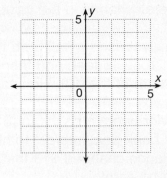

Describe how to locate each point.

27. (21, −36) _____

28. (−14, −25) _____

29. Geometry Plot these points: (−1, 1), (2, 5), (5, 1), (2, −3).

   a. Connect the points to form a quadrilateral.

   b. Classify the quadrilateral in as many ways as possible.

_____

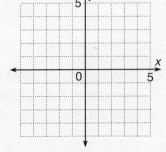

Graphing Slides and Flips

For Exercises 1–2, use the point $P(2, -1)$ to plot and label P'.

1. Slide P 2 units left and 3 units up.

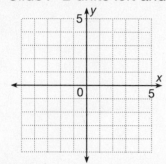

2. Reflect P across the x-axis.

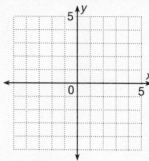

For Exercises 3–4, plot the image of quadrilateral $GHIJ$.

3. Translate $GHIJ$ 2 units right and 2 units down.

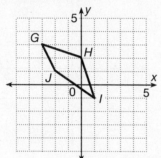

4. Slide $GHIJ$ 4 units right and 2 units up.

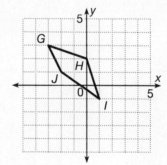

5. $\triangle ABC$ has vertices at $A(-3, 4)$, $B(1, 3)$, and $C(-2, 0)$.

a. Draw the graph of $\triangle ABC$.

b. Create $\triangle A'B'C'$ by translating $\triangle ABC$ 3 units right and 4 units down.

c. Give the coordinates of the vertices of $\triangle A'B'C'$.

A' _____ B' _____ C' _____

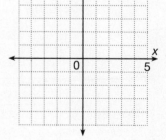

6. $\triangle LMN$ has vertices at $L(-2, 4)$, $M(1, 2)$, and $N(-4, -1)$.

a. Draw the graph of $\triangle LMN$.

b. Create $\triangle L'M'N'$ by reflecting $\triangle LMN$ across the y-axis.

c. Give the coordinates of the vertices of $\triangle L'M'N'$.

L' _____ M' _____ N' _____

Graphing Equations

For Exercises 1–4, make a T-table with five (x, y) pairs for each.

1. $y = x + 12$ **2.** $y = -8x$ **3.** $y = x - 20$ **4.** $y = 15x$

Graph each equation.

5. $y = x - 1$

6. $y = x + 5$

7. $y = -2$

8. $y = -3x$

9. $y = x - 2$

10. $y = 2 - x$

11. The Mystery Music Company sells "grab bag" cassettes for $1 each. There is a shipping charge of $4 per order. The equation for the cost of an order is $y = x + 4$. Graph this equation.

Name _____

Section 9B Review

For Exercises 1–3, use the coordinate grid.

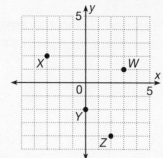

1. What are the coordinates of each point?

   W _____   X _____

   Y _____   Z _____

2. If point Y were translated left 3 units and down
   2 units, what would be the coordinates of Y′?   _____

3. If point X were reflected across the x-axis, what
   would be the coordinates of X′?   _____

Graph each equation.

4. $y = 4x$

5. $y = x + 3$

6. $y = 4$

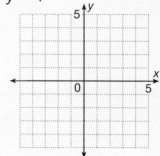

7. **Geometry** The coordinates of two opposite vertices of a square
   are $(-1, -1)$ and $(-4, 2)$. If the square is reflected across the
   y-axis, what are the coordinates of the four vertices of its image?

   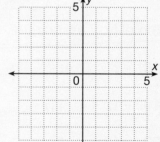

   _____

8. Graph the lines $y = -3$ and $y = 4 - x$.
   Do the lines have a point in common? Explain.

   _____

9. **Career** Drafters use a tool shaped like a triangle to make
   accurate drawings. If the base of this tool has length 4.25 in.
   and the height is 8.23 in., what is the area? *[Lesson 4-6]*   _____

10. Classify the shape of the sign in as many ways as possible.
    [Lesson 8-7]

    _____

    _____

Name _____

Cumulative Review Chapters 1–9

Find the circumference C and the area A of each circle where
r = radius and d = diameter. Use 3.14 for π. *[Lessons 4-7, 4-8]*

1. $r = 7$ cm, $C \approx$ _____ ,

$A \approx$ _____

2. $d = 10$ ft, $C \approx$ _____ ,

$A \approx$ _____

3. $r = 11$ in., $C \approx$ _____ ,

$A \approx$ _____

4. $r = 7.3$ m, $C \approx$ _____ ,

$A \approx$ _____

Subtract. Write the answer as a whole or mixed number in lowest terms. *[Lesson 6-6]*

5. $9\frac{1}{4} - 6\frac{1}{8}$ _____

6. $3\frac{1}{2} - 1\frac{1}{3}$ _____

7. $4\frac{1}{5} - 3\frac{1}{4}$ _____

8. $7\frac{5}{8} - 5\frac{1}{2}$ _____

9. $6\frac{1}{3} - 2\frac{3}{4}$ _____

10. $7\frac{2}{3} - 4\frac{1}{6}$ _____

11. $4\frac{3}{5} - 4\frac{1}{10}$ _____

12. $3\frac{1}{3} - \frac{1}{5}$ _____

13. $8\frac{1}{4} - 5\frac{4}{5}$ _____

Classify each figure in as many ways as possible. *[Lesson 8-7]*

14. _____

_____

15. _____

_____

Simplify. *[Lessons 9-2, 9-3, 9-4]*

16. $7 \times (-4)$ _____

17. $10 - 17$ _____

18. $21 \div (-7)$ _____

19. $-12 + (-11)$ _____

20. $3 \times (-8)$ _____

21. $8 - (-9)$ _____

22. $-48 \div (-6)$ _____

23. $-4 + 22$ _____

24. -5×8 _____

Plot and label each point. *[Lesson 9-5]*

25. $W(-3, -2)$

26. $H(1, -3)$

27. $L(2, -5)$

28. $M(3, 2)$

29. $B(-2, 4)$

30. $D(-4, 0)$

31. $G(4, 3)$

32. $Q(-1, 1)$

33. $Z(4, -3)$

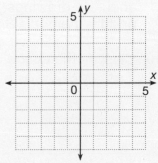

Name _____

What is a Ratio?

For Exercises 1–4, use the shapes pictured.

1. What is the ratio of triangles to circles? _____

2. What is the ratio of triangles to stars? _____

3. Give the ratio of circles to squares. _____

4. What is the ratio of triangles to the whole group? _____

A box contains 6 green chips, 10 blue chips, and 7 white chips.
Give each ratio in three ways.

5. Green chips to blue chips

_____

6. Blue chips to white chips

_____

7. White chips to green chips

_____

8. Green chips to white chips

_____

For Exercises 9–11, refer to the animals pictured.

9. The ratio of which animal to the whole group is 4 : 15?

_____

10. The ratio of which animal to the whole group is 1 : 5?

_____

11. Which two animals are compared in a ratio of $\frac{4}{3}$?

_____

12. **Social Science** In 1995, the U.S. Senate consisted of 46 Democrats and 54 Republicans.

   a. Give the ratio of Democrats to Republicans in lowest terms. _____

   b. Give the ratio of Republicans to all Senators in lowest terms. _____

13. At Jackson High School, 14 out of 35 students in the marching band are sophomores. Write this as a ratio in lowest terms. _____

Name _____

Equal Ratios

Give two ratios equal to the given ratio.

1. 8 to 12 _____

2. $\frac{3}{5}$ _____

3. 9 to 3 _____

4. 15 : 35 _____

5. $\frac{8}{10}$ _____

6. $\frac{7}{8}$ _____

State if the ratios are equal.

7. 4 : 8; 1 : 2 _____

8. $\frac{3}{6}$, $\frac{5}{8}$ _____

9. 12 to 15, 4 to 5 _____

10. $\frac{10}{12}$, $\frac{15}{18}$ _____

11. 15 : 20, 20 : 25 _____

12. 10 to 8, 20 to 15 _____

13. $\frac{5}{9}$, 8 to 13 _____

14. 8 : 14, $\frac{4}{7}$ _____

15. 12 to 28, 18 : 42 _____

For exercises 16–19, give three equal ratios.

16. A third grade class has 4 boys for every 3 girls. _____

17. A pet store has 5 cat collars for every 8 dog collars. _____

18. A corporation has 2 secretaries for every executive. _____

19. A carnival game has 2 winners for every 7 losers. _____

Complete each table of equal ratios.

20. 8 snakes for every 3 turtles

Snakes				
Turtles	3	6	9	12

21. 7 dogs out of 12 pets

Dogs	7		21	
Pets		24		48

22. 12 pizzas to 9 lasagnas

Pizzas	4	8		
Lasagnas			9	12

23. 16 cars to 20 trucks

Cars			12	16
Trucks	5	10		

24. Social Science The ratio of Delaware residents to Maine residents was about 55 : 100 in 1970 and about 66 : 120 in 1990. Are these ratios equal? _____

What is a Rate?

State if the ratio is a unit rate.

1. $\dfrac{3 \text{ cats}}{5 \text{ dogs}}$ _____

2. $\dfrac{1 \text{ ounce}}{\$0.15}$ _____

3. $\dfrac{12 \text{ inches}}{1 \text{ foot}}$ _____

4. $\dfrac{20 \text{ miles}}{1 \text{ hour}}$ _____

5. $\dfrac{6 \text{ pounds}}{1 \text{ dollar}}$ _____

6. $\dfrac{125 \text{ miles}}{5 \text{ hours}}$ _____

7. $\dfrac{1 \text{ table}}{6 \text{ chairs}}$ _____

8. $\dfrac{1 \text{ dollar}}{3 \text{ oranges}}$ _____

9. $\dfrac{2 \text{ cups}}{1 \text{ pint}}$ _____

10. $\dfrac{3 \text{ quarts}}{2 \text{ pounds}}$ _____

11. $\dfrac{4 \text{ books}}{1 \text{ dollar}}$ _____

12. $\dfrac{13 \text{ feet}}{1 \text{ foot}}$ _____

For each situation, give two equal rates.

13. Robert drove 20 miles in 30 minutes.

_____

14. Helen earned $18 for working 3 hours.

_____

15. A radio station played 15 songs in 1 hour.

_____

16. A breakfast cereal contains 75 raisins in every pound.

_____

17. Becky ran 2 miles in 14 minutes.

_____

18. June bought 3 pounds of asparagus for $2.

_____

For Exercises 19–21, use the bar graph.

19. Give a rate that uses the number 28.

Year: _____   Rate: _____

20. Give three different rates that describe the average fuel efficiency in 1985.

_____

Fuel Efficiency of Average U.S. Passenger Car

21. Use the average fuel efficiency in 1990 to give a rate that compares a distance to $\frac{1}{3}$ gallon of gasoline. _____

22. Rhoda has 4 hours to type a 12-page report. How much time can she spend typing each page? _____

23. Helga did 3 math problems in 5 minutes. If there are 45 similar problems in her homework assignment, how long will it take her to complete the assignment? _____

Section 10A Review

1. About 160,000 of Rhode Island's 1,000,000 residents live in Providence. Write this ratio in lowest terms. _____

2. Last week a local humane society rescued 14 dogs and 10 cats.Give each ratio in lowest terms.

   a. Dogs to cats _____   **b.** Cats to dogs _____

   c. Dogs to all animals _____   **d.** Cats to all animals _____

3. Lucy has 5 quarters, 3 dimes, and 2 nickels. Give 5 ratios in lowest terms to describe the situation.

   _____

   _____

4. Complete each table of equal ratios.

Men	7	21	49	70
Women	9			

Telephones	5	10		
Fax Machines		12	18	24

5. Give three ratios equal to 45 : 65. _____

6. There are 8 magazines and 15 books. Write the ratio of magazines to books in three ways. _____

For Exercises 7–8, use the figures pictured.

7. Give the ratio of circles to hexagons. _____

8. What is the ratio of hexagons and squares to circles? _____

9. Martin watched 10 movies in 25 hours. Write this as a rate in lowest terms. _____

10. The Peachy King Beverage Company advertises that its product contains "$\frac{2}{5}$ real fruit juice!" How much fruit juice is in a 16 ounce container of this drink? *[Lesson 7-2]* _____

11. **Science** An emperor penguin has been observed diving to a depth of 1584 feet below sea level. Write an integer to describe the penguin's height during its dive. *[Lesson 9-1]* _____

Name _____

What is a Proportion?

State whether or not each pair of ratios forms a proportion.

1. $\frac{6}{12} \stackrel{?}{=} \frac{12}{14}$ _____ 2. $\frac{3}{20} \stackrel{?}{=} \frac{2}{10}$ _____ 3. $\frac{20}{12} \stackrel{?}{=} \frac{25}{15}$ _____

4. $\frac{27}{6} \stackrel{?}{=} \frac{36}{8}$ _____ 5. $\frac{13}{11} \stackrel{?}{=} \frac{24}{20}$ _____ 6. $\frac{3}{4} \stackrel{?}{=} \frac{15}{20}$ _____

7. $\frac{10}{4} \stackrel{?}{=} \frac{45}{20}$ _____ 8. $\frac{15}{10} \stackrel{?}{=} \frac{3}{2}$ _____ 9. $\frac{12}{21} \stackrel{?}{=} \frac{16}{28}$ _____

10. $\frac{3}{24} \stackrel{?}{=} \frac{4}{32}$ _____ 11. $\frac{12}{20} \stackrel{?}{=} \frac{4}{7}$ _____ 12. $\frac{2}{9} \stackrel{?}{=} \frac{5}{22}$ _____

13. $\frac{6}{15} \stackrel{?}{=} \frac{4}{12}$ _____ 14. $\frac{15}{18} \stackrel{?}{=} \frac{20}{24}$ _____ 15. $\frac{17}{12} \stackrel{?}{=} \frac{10}{7}$ _____

16. $\frac{25}{35} \stackrel{?}{=} \frac{15}{21}$ _____ 17. $\frac{10}{9} \stackrel{?}{=} \frac{16}{14}$ _____ 18. $\frac{32}{36} \stackrel{?}{=} \frac{40}{45}$ _____

19. $\frac{2 \text{ tsp}}{7 \text{ gal}} \stackrel{?}{=} \frac{6 \text{ tsp}}{21 \text{ gal}}$ ___ 20. $\frac{12 \text{ cm}}{20 \text{ g}} \stackrel{?}{=} \frac{15 \text{ g}}{25 \text{ cm}}$ ___ 21. $\frac{\$14}{3 \text{ hr}} \stackrel{?}{=} \frac{\$84}{18 \text{ hr}}$ ___

22. $\frac{27 \text{ lb}}{\$21} \stackrel{?}{=} \frac{14 \text{ lb}}{\$18}$ ___ 23. $\frac{15 \text{ sec}}{21 \text{ sec}} \stackrel{?}{=} \frac{10 \text{ in.}}{15 \text{ in.}}$ ___ 24. $\frac{6 \text{ ft}}{13 \text{ gal}} \stackrel{?}{=} \frac{7 \text{ ft}}{14 \text{ gal}}$ ___

For Exercises 25–30, choose the proportion that is written correctly.

25. a. $\frac{20 \text{ men}}{25 \text{ women}} = \frac{5 \text{ men}}{4 \text{ women}}$ b. $\frac{20 \text{ men}}{25 \text{ women}} = \frac{4 \text{ men}}{5 \text{ women}}$ c. $\frac{4 \text{ men}}{5 \text{ women}} = \frac{25 \text{ women}}{20 \text{ men}}$

26. a. $\frac{27 \text{ acres}}{\$15} = \frac{\$25}{45 \text{ acres}}$ b. $\frac{\$27}{15 \text{ acres}} = \frac{\$25}{45 \text{ acres}}$ c. $\frac{45 \text{ acres}}{\$25} = \frac{27 \text{ acres}}{\$15}$

27. a. $\frac{12 \text{ pies}}{4 \text{ cakes}} = \frac{6 \text{ cakes}}{18 \text{ pies}}$ b. $\frac{4 \text{ cakes}}{12 \text{ pies}} = \frac{6 \text{ cakes}}{18 \text{ pies}}$ c. $\frac{12 \text{ pies}}{4 \text{ cakes}} = \frac{6 \text{ pies}}{18 \text{ cakes}}$

28. a. $\frac{6 \text{ gal}}{15 \text{ gal}} = \frac{2 \text{ min}}{5 \text{ min}}$ b. $\frac{5 \text{ min}}{15 \text{ gal}} = \frac{6 \text{ gal}}{2 \text{ min}}$ c. $\frac{6 \text{ gal}}{2 \text{ min}} = \frac{5 \text{ gal}}{15 \text{ min}}$

29. a. $\frac{25 \text{ chairs}}{5 \text{ tables}} = \frac{10 \text{ tables}}{2 \text{ chairs}}$ b. $\frac{25 \text{ chairs}}{5 \text{ tables}} = \frac{2 \text{ tables}}{10 \text{ chairs}}$ c. $\frac{25 \text{ chairs}}{5 \text{ tables}} = \frac{10 \text{ chairs}}{2 \text{ tables}}$

30. a. $\frac{36 \text{ lb}}{28 \text{ ft}} = \frac{18 \text{ lb}}{14 \text{ ft}}$ b. $\frac{18 \text{ lb}}{14 \text{ ft}} = \frac{28 \text{ lb}}{36 \text{ ft}}$ c $\frac{36 \text{ ft}}{28 \text{ lb}} = \frac{18 \text{ lb}}{14 \text{ ft}}$

31. During the butterfly stroke competitions at the 1972 Summer Olympic Games, Mayumi Aoki swam 100 meters in 64 seconds, and Karen Moe swam 200 meters in 136 seconds. Do these rates form a proportion? _____

32. At Deliah's Hardware, you can buy 5 feet of PVC pipe for $1.10, or 8 feet for $1.76. Are these prices proportional?

Solving Proportions Using Cross Products

Solve each proportion.

1. $\dfrac{12}{a} = \dfrac{16}{20}$

a = _____

2. $\dfrac{2}{8} = \dfrac{t}{20}$

t = _____

3. $\dfrac{30}{a} = \dfrac{20}{18}$

a = _____

4. $\dfrac{45}{x} = \dfrac{18}{8}$

x = _____

5. $\dfrac{u}{5} = \dfrac{6}{3}$

u = _____

6. $\dfrac{15}{5} = \dfrac{6}{a}$

a = _____

7. $\dfrac{m}{8} = \dfrac{12}{16}$

m = _____

8. $\dfrac{40}{y} = \dfrac{16}{2}$

y = _____

9. $\dfrac{16}{36} = \dfrac{g}{45}$

g = _____

10. $\dfrac{s}{28} = \dfrac{30}{21}$

s = _____

11. $\dfrac{4}{5} = \dfrac{8}{d}$

d = _____

12. $\dfrac{15}{5} = \dfrac{12}{c}$

c = _____

13. $\dfrac{16}{28} = \dfrac{h}{7}$

h = _____

14. $\dfrac{2}{k} = \dfrac{3}{6}$

k = _____

15. $\dfrac{30}{3} = \dfrac{j}{2}$

j = _____

16. $\dfrac{3}{r} = \dfrac{2}{8}$

r = _____

17. $\dfrac{20}{8} = \dfrac{f}{2}$

f = _____

18. $\dfrac{2}{20} = \dfrac{z}{10}$

z = _____

19. $\dfrac{20}{d} = \dfrac{4}{5}$

d = _____

20. $\dfrac{4}{q} = \dfrac{2}{7}$

q = _____

21. $\dfrac{z}{15} = \dfrac{2}{6}$

z = _____

22. $\dfrac{2}{3} = \dfrac{b}{6}$

b = _____

23. $\dfrac{y}{2} = \dfrac{6}{4}$

y = _____

24. $\dfrac{2}{5} = \dfrac{4}{n}$

n = _____

25. $\dfrac{10}{m} = \dfrac{8}{4}$

m = _____

26. $\dfrac{27}{6} = \dfrac{j}{8}$

j = _____

27. $\dfrac{g}{3.5} = \dfrac{1.6}{1.4}$

g = _____

28. $\dfrac{8}{36} = \dfrac{p}{9}$

p = _____

29. $\dfrac{14}{16} = \dfrac{28}{p}$

p = _____

30. $\dfrac{t}{24} = \dfrac{10}{16}$

t = _____

31. $\dfrac{45}{u} = \dfrac{27}{12}$

u = _____

32. $\dfrac{10}{45} = \dfrac{2}{x}$

x = _____

33. $\dfrac{25}{q} = \dfrac{15}{12}$

q = _____

34. $\dfrac{15}{20} = \dfrac{v}{4}$

v = _____

35. $\dfrac{p}{6} = \dfrac{3}{2}$

p = _____

36. $\dfrac{3}{7} = \dfrac{12}{a}$

a = _____

37. **Measurement** If 5 pints of water weigh 80 oz, find the weight of 12 pints of water.

_____

38. In 1967, a minimum wage worker would receive $84 for 60 hours of work. How much would the worker receive for 75 hours of work?

_____

Solving Proportions Using Unit Rates

Find the unit rate for each.

1. $\dfrac{12 \text{ books}}{3 \text{ shelves}}$ _____

2. $\dfrac{14 \text{ tsp}}{7 \text{ gal}}$ _____

3. $\dfrac{108 \text{ pages}}{9 \text{ hours}}$ _____

4. $\dfrac{6 \text{ gal}}{2 \text{ min}}$ _____

5. $\dfrac{30.48 \text{ cm}}{12 \text{ in.}}$ _____

6. $\dfrac{40 \text{ mice}}{8 \text{ rats}}$ _____

7. $\dfrac{28 \text{ cats}}{4 \text{ dogs}}$ _____

8. $\dfrac{\$315}{35 \text{ hr}}$ _____

9. $\dfrac{10 \text{ CDs}}{5 \text{ tapes}}$ _____

10. $\dfrac{90 \text{ cars}}{15 \text{ trucks}}$ _____

11. $\dfrac{14 \text{ cups}}{42 \text{ sec}}$ _____

12. $\dfrac{18 \text{ boys}}{18 \text{ girls}}$ _____

13. $\dfrac{576 \text{ pt}}{72 \text{ gal}}$ _____

14. $\dfrac{120 \text{ mi}}{3 \text{ hr}}$ _____

15. $\dfrac{35 \text{ carrots}}{10 \text{ potatoes}}$ _____

16. $\dfrac{36 \text{ cups}}{18 \text{ bowls}}$ _____

17. $\dfrac{68 \text{ men}}{17 \text{ women}}$ _____

18. $\dfrac{375 \text{ ft}^2}{25 \text{ people}}$ _____

Solve each proportion using unit rates.

19. $\dfrac{}{20 \text{ moose}} = \dfrac{14 \text{ cows}}{10 \text{ moose}}$

20. $\dfrac{25 \text{ pt}}{10 \text{ ft}^2} = \dfrac{}{8 \text{ ft}^2}$

21. $\dfrac{7 \text{ hits}}{2 \text{ innings}} = \dfrac{}{6 \text{ innings}}$

22. $\dfrac{4 \text{ ft}}{12 \text{ sec}} = \dfrac{}{6 \text{ sec}}$

23. $\dfrac{\$15}{9 \text{ lb}} = \dfrac{}{3 \text{ lb}}$

24. $\dfrac{15 \text{ meals}}{3 \text{ days}} = \dfrac{}{5 \text{ days}}$

25. $\dfrac{5 \text{ drops}}{50 \text{ gal}} = \dfrac{}{30 \text{ gal}}$

26. $\dfrac{}{2 \text{ hr}} = \dfrac{15°}{3 \text{ hr}}$

27. $\dfrac{}{4 \text{ hr}} = \dfrac{16 \text{ gal}}{2 \text{ hr}}$

28. $\dfrac{45 \text{ in.}}{5 \text{ lb}} = \dfrac{}{2 \text{ lb}}$

29. $\dfrac{12 \text{ lb}}{4 \text{ sec}} = \dfrac{}{1 \text{ sec}}$

30. $\dfrac{\$6}{2 \text{ hr}} = \dfrac{}{3 \text{ hr}}$

31. $\dfrac{35 \text{ mi}}{10 \text{ L}} = \dfrac{}{8 \text{ L}}$

32. $\dfrac{}{4 \text{ in}^3} = \dfrac{21 \text{ oz}}{6 \text{ in}^3}$

33. $\dfrac{27 \text{ min}}{24 \text{ ft}} = \dfrac{}{8 \text{ ft}}$

34. In 1909, French workmen removed a white stork's nest weighing 660 kilograms from the top of a cathedral. The nest also weighed 1452 pounds. Using these measurements, find the number of pounds in a kilogram. _____

35. **History** The Northrop XB–35 aircraft used in World War II had a wingspan of 172 feet. Melba's model of this aircraft has a wingspan of $21\frac{1}{2}$ inches. How many feet does one inch of the model represent? _____

Similar Figures

Find the missing side lengths.

1. A = _____ B = _____ C = _____

9 in.   12 in.
12 in.   A   C
              B

2. A = _____ B = _____

A   22.5 cm   14 cm   17.5 cm
     B   10.5 cm

3. A = _____ B = _____ C = _____

A
3 m   B   4 m   4 m
   C   4 m
                  4 m

4. A = _____ B = _____ C = _____

4 in.   A
$2\frac{1}{2}$ in. $2\frac{1}{2}$ in. $7\frac{1}{2}$ in.   B
   4 in.
                         C

5. A = _____ B = _____

        18 ft
   10 ft
A 9 ft
   B   14 ft

6. A = _____ B = _____ C = _____

            2.5 cm   B
6.5 cm   6 cm A   C
       5 cm
            6 cm

7. On the map, 1 inch equals 850 actual miles.

a. What are the actual distances between the cities?

New York to New Orleans

_____

New Orleans to Miami

_____

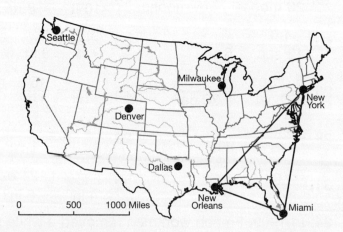

Miami to New York

_____

b. Is the triangle shown on the map similar to the life-size triangle? Explain.

_____

8. The lengths of the sides of a triangle are 45 cm, 55 cm, and 70 cm. The shortest side of a similar triangle has length 27 cm. What are the lengths of the other two sides of the similar triangle?

_____

Section 10B Review

Find the unit rate for each ratio.

1. $\dfrac{45 \text{ kg}}{15 \text{ m}}$ _____

2. $\dfrac{48 \text{ lemons}}{\$8}$ _____

3. $\dfrac{105 \text{ mi}}{3 \text{ hr}}$ _____

4. $\dfrac{108 \text{ cows}}{6 \text{ acres}}$ _____

5. $\dfrac{20 \text{ windows}}{4 \text{ doors}}$ _____

6. $\dfrac{100 \text{ cars}}{25 \text{ min}}$ _____

Solve each proportion.

7. $\dfrac{15}{} = \dfrac{3}{10}$

8. $\dfrac{3}{18} = \dfrac{2}{}$

9. $\dfrac{}{12} = \dfrac{21}{18}$

10. $\dfrac{4 \text{ dogs}}{9 \text{ cats}} = \dfrac{}{18 \text{ cats}}$

11. $\dfrac{18 \text{ rings}}{\$20} = \dfrac{}{\$30}$

12. $\dfrac{25 \text{ gal}}{5 \text{ min}} = \dfrac{}{4 \text{ min}}$

13. In 1996, a chocolate chip cookie with an area of 5240 square feet was made by Cookie Time of New Zealand. It contained about 5600 pounds of chocolate. This equals how many pounds of chocolate per square foot of cookie?

_____

14. If Chester can type 75 words in 100 seconds, how many words could he type in 5 minutes?

_____

In each pair of similar figures, find the missing side lengths.

15. $A =$ _____ $B =$ _____ $C =$ _____   **16.** $A =$ _____ $B =$ _____

27 in.
45 in. 45 in.   21 in.
27 in.   A C
         B

8.5 cm 7.5 cm   A 12 cm
4 cm   B

17. An instant pasta dinner package contains a packet of plain pasta plus a flavor packet weighing $\frac{1}{8}$ pound. If the entire package weighs $\frac{7}{16}$ pound, what is the weight of the plain pasta? *[Lesson 6-3]*

_____

18. Mildred always has $200 of her monthly salary transferred automatically to a savings account. The equation $y = x - 200$ gives the amount of her paycheck, where x is her after-tax income. Graph this equation. *[Lesson 9-7]*

Name _____

What is a Percent?

Give the percent of each figure that is shaded.

1. _____

2. _____

3. _____

4. _____

5. _____

6. _____

7. _____

8. _____

9. _____

The circle graph shows the educational attainment of Americans over 25 years old in 1994. Use the graph for Exercises 10–12.

Educational Attainment of Americans

Less than 4 years of high school, 19%

4 years of college or more, 22%

4 years of high school but less than 4 years of college, 59%

10. What percent of the population has completed

less than 4 years of high school? _____

4 years of high school or more? _____

11. Which category includes the highest percent of Americans over 25?

_____

What is the percent? _____

12. Which two categories combined amount for 41% of Americans over 25?

_____

13. **Geography** 22% of the land in Vietnam is arable (suitable for farming). What percent is not arable?

_____

Estimating Percents

Estimate what percent of each figure is shaded.

1. _____

2. _____

3. _____

4. _____

5. _____

6. _____

7. _____

8. _____

9. _____

Estimate the percent.

10. 13 out of 66 _____   **11.** 31 out of 118 _____   **12.** 18 out of 21 _____

13. 73 out of 80 _____   **14.** 47 out of 77 _____   **15.** 93 out of 190 _____

16. $\dfrac{312}{420}$ _____   **17.** $\dfrac{59}{84}$ _____   **18.** $\dfrac{25}{240}$ _____   **19.** $\dfrac{45}{148}$ _____

20. $\dfrac{59}{74}$ _____   **21.** $\dfrac{88}{116}$ _____   **22.** $\dfrac{41}{47}$ _____   **23.** $\dfrac{61}{99}$ _____

24. In 1989, the EarthGrains Bakery in Fort Payne, Alabama, set a world record by baking a cake weighing 128,000 lb. The cake included 16,000 lb of icing. About what percent of the cake was icing?

_____

25. Patents are issued to inventors to prevent others from stealing their ideas. In 1965, 37,000 out of 63,000 patents were issued to U.S. corporations. About what percent is this?

_____

Converting Percents to Fractions and Decimals

Convert to a fraction in lowest terms.

1. 80% _____   **2.** 25% _____   **3.** 78% _____   **4.** 98% _____

5. 32% _____   **6.** 30% _____   **7.** 45% _____   **8.** 118% _____

9. 65% _____   **10.** 185% _____   **11.** 63% _____   **12.** 28% _____

13. 275% _____   **14.** 84% _____   **15.** 104% _____   **16.** 18% _____

Convert to a percent.

17. $\frac{7}{10}$ _____   **18.** $\frac{37}{50}$ _____   **19.** $\frac{1}{2}$ _____   **20.** $\frac{18}{25}$ _____

21. 0.41 _____   **22.** 0.03 _____   **23.** 0.74 _____   **24.** 0.92 _____

25. $\frac{123}{300}$ _____   **26.** $\frac{15}{20}$ _____   **27.** $\frac{31}{20}$ _____   **28.** $\frac{1}{10}$ _____

29. 0.67 _____   **30.** 4.10 _____   **31.** 0.8 _____   **32.** 0.137 _____

Give the shaded part of each figure as a percent, fraction, and decimal.

33.   percent: _____

fraction: _____

decimal: _____

34. percent: _____

fraction: _____

decimal: _____

35.   percent: _____

fraction: _____

decimal: _____

36.   percent: _____

fraction: _____

decimal: _____

37. In 1993, about $\frac{1}{50}$ of American children lived with relatives other than their parents. Convert this value to a percent.

_____

38. In 1950, $\frac{2}{25}$ of the American population was at least 65 years old. What percent is this?

_____

Finding a Percent of a Whole Number

Simplify. Round your answer to the nearest hundredth.

1. 28% of 11 _____   **2.** 44% of 46 _____   **3.** 66% of 21 _____

4. 95% of 49 _____   **5.** 12% of 8 _____   **6.** 14% of 37 _____

7. 29% of $16.50 _____   **8.** 1% of 32 _____   **9.** 15% of 60 _____

10. 42% of 4 _____   **11.** 17% of 2.89 _____   **12.** 39% of 83.75 _____

13. 11% of 18 _____   **14.** 3% of 15 _____   **15.** 24% of 100 _____

16. 20% of 7.63 _____   **17.** 19% of $21.95 _____   **18.** 6% of 53 _____

19. 36% of 21 _____   **20.** 30% of 69 _____   **21.** 35% of 35 _____

22. 61% of 41 _____   **23.** 7% of 12.8 _____   **24.** 68% of 84 _____

25. 9% of 64.88 _____   **26.** 56% of 98 _____   **27.** 73% of 79 _____

Find the total amount.

28. 24% of _____ is 38.4   **29.** 30% of _____ is 14.4   **30.** 16% of _____ is 52

31. 79% of ____ is 402.9   **32.** 41% of _____ is 24.6   **33.** 38% of _____ is 114

34. 5% of _____ is 14.25   **35.** 84% of ____ is $74.76   **36.** 62% of _____ is 775

37. 55% of _____ is 40.7   **38.** 25% of _____ is 21   **39.** 12% of _____ is 10.32

40. 36% of _____ is 63   **41.** 8% of _____ is 9.6   **42.** 68% of _____ is $17

43. 65% of ____ is 140.4   **44.** 32% of _____ is 12   **45.** 88% of _____ is 132

46. Consumer Molly bought a video game that was priced
at $24.95. She had to pay 6.5% sales tax. Find the sales
tax amount and the total price.

tax: _____   total: _____

47. The population of Chula Vista, California increased
from 83,927 in 1980 to 135,163 in 1990. Find the
percent increase.

_____

Name _____

Section 10C Review

Estimate the percent of each figure that is shaded.

1. _____ 2. _____ 3. _____

Convert each percent to a decimal and a fraction.

4. 37% _____ **5.** 40% _____ **6.** 84% _____

7. 35% _____ **8.** 170% _____ **9.** 12% _____

10. 68% _____ **11.** 8% _____ **12.** 38% _____

Convert to a percent.

13. 0.47 _____ **14.** 0.1 _____ **15.** 0.95 _____ **16.** 0.74 _____

17. $\frac{7}{10}$ _____ **18.** $\frac{19}{25}$ _____ **19.** $\frac{14}{40}$ _____ **20.** $\frac{27}{50}$ _____

21. 0.02 _____ **22.** 2.73 _____ **23.** 0.462 _____ **24.** 0.87 _____

25. $\frac{11}{2}$ _____ **26.** $\frac{8}{5}$ _____ **27.** $\frac{9}{10}$ _____ **28.** $\frac{8}{25}$ _____

Simplify.

29. 28% of 64 _____ **30.** 70% of 51 _____ **31.** 68% of 94 _____

32. 43% of 83 _____ **33.** 4% of 23 _____ **34.** 86% of 28.5 _____

35. 225% of 74 _____ **36.** 94% of 46 _____ **37.** 63% of 37 _____

38. Measurement One grain is to equal $\frac{1}{20}$ of a scruple. Write and solve an equation to find the number of scruples in 70 grains. *[Lesson 7-6]*

_____

39. Science Temperatures on Mercury are as high as 510°C and as low as −210°C. Find the difference between these temperatures. *[Lesson 9-3]*

_____

Name _____

Cumulative Review Chapters 1–10

Write in lowest terms. *[Lesson 5-5]*

1. $\frac{9}{15}$ _____ **2.** $\frac{20}{25}$ _____ **3.** $\frac{24}{36}$ _____ **4.** $\frac{10}{22}$ _____

5. $\frac{14}{49}$ _____ **6.** $\frac{8}{64}$ _____ **7.** $\frac{6}{21}$ _____ **8.** $\frac{12}{90}$ _____

9. $\frac{35}{75}$ _____ **10.** $\frac{24}{42}$ _____ **11.** $\frac{8}{18}$ _____ **12.** $\frac{33}{57}$ _____

Simplify. *[Lessons 7-3, 7-5]*

13. $3\frac{2}{7} \times 2\frac{2}{3}$ _____ **14.** $\frac{1}{9} \div 6\frac{2}{3}$ _____ **15.** $4\frac{4}{5} \times 1\frac{1}{5}$ _____ **16.** $\frac{2}{3} \div \frac{1}{3}$ _____

17. $5\frac{1}{2} \times \frac{1}{4}$ _____ **18.** $1\frac{5}{6} \div \frac{3}{10}$ _____ **19.** $1\frac{2}{3} \times 1\frac{1}{4}$ _____ **20.** $7\frac{1}{2} \div 4$ _____

21. $\frac{5}{7} \times \frac{14}{15}$ _____ **22.** $\frac{5}{7} \div 2\frac{2}{3}$ _____ **23.** $1\frac{1}{5} \times 4\frac{1}{3}$ _____ **24.** $4\frac{1}{2} \div 12\frac{1}{2}$ _____

Classify each triangle as acute, right, or obtuse. *[Lesson 8-4]*

25. _____ **26.** _____ **27.** _____ **28.** _____

Solve each proportion. *[Lesson 10-5]*

29. $\frac{45}{50} = \frac{d}{40}$ **30.** $\frac{10}{2} = \frac{j}{5}$ **31.** $\frac{15}{12} = \frac{y}{8}$ **32.** $\frac{y}{6} = \frac{15}{9}$

$d =$ _____ $j =$ _____ $y =$ _____ $y =$ _____

33. $\frac{12}{16} = \frac{q}{20}$ **34.** $\frac{35}{15} = \frac{7}{g}$ **35.** $\frac{27}{m} = \frac{9}{7}$ **36.** $\frac{8}{12} = \frac{4}{d}$

$q =$ _____ $g =$ _____ $m =$ _____ $d =$ _____

Find the total amount. *[Lesson 10-11]*

37. 18% of _____ is 117 **38.** 35% of _____ is 77 **39.** 70% of _____ is 33.6

40. 75% of _____ is 96 **41.** 62% of _____ is 186 **42.** 44% of _____ is 121

43. 63% of _____ is 113.4 **44.** 120% of _____ is 102 **45.** 185% of _____ is 74

Name _____

Classifying Solids

Classify each solid. If it is a polyhedron, tell how many vertices, edges,
and faces it has.

1. _____

V: ___ E: ___ F: ___

2. _____

V: ___ E: ___ F: ___

3. _____

V: ___ E: ___ F: ___

4. _____

V: ___ E: ___ F: ___

5. _____

V: ___ E: ___ F: ___

6. _____

V: ___ E: ___ F: ___

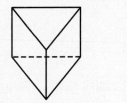

Draw an example of each.

7. Cube

8. Square pyramid

9. Rectangular prism

Classify each group of figures.

10. _____

11. _____

12. _____

Exploring Surface Area

Find the area of each net. Classify the solid.

1. SA: _____

2. SA: _____

Each side is 4.5 cm

3. SA: _____

State the number of faces. Then classify each face and find the total surface area.

4. _____

SA: _____

5. _____

SA: _____

6. _____

SA: _____

7. _____

SA: _____

8. _____

SA: _____

9. _____

SA: _____

10. A box of shredded wheat cereal measures 7 in. by $9\frac{3}{4}$ in. by $2\frac{1}{4}$ in. How much cardboard was used to make the box? (Assume there is no overlap.) _____

Name _____

Surface Area Formulas

Find the surface area.

1. _____

11 in.
11 in.
11 in.

2. _____

5 cm
13 cm
8 cm

3. _____

15 yd
11 yd
11 yd

4. _____

23 mm
23 mm   23 mm

5. _____

6 ft
5 ft
9 ft

6. _____

8 m
8 m   5 m

7. _____

$5\frac{1}{4}$ in.
$5\frac{1}{4}$ in.
$5\frac{1}{4}$ in.

8. _____

21 cm
37 cm
6 cm

9. _____

16 yd
6 yd
6 yd

10. _____

42 m
42 m
42 m

11. _____

4 ft
2 ft
1 ft

12. _____

4.1 m
2.3 m
2.3 m

13. _____

13 in.
13 in.   13 in.

14. _____

5.8 cm
18.0 cm
10.5 cm

15. _____

$11\frac{1}{4}$ in.
$7\frac{1}{4}$ in.
$7\frac{1}{4}$ in.

16. _____

3.4 mm
3.4 mm
3.4 mm

Find the surface area of each rectangular prism.

17. $l = 9$ ft, $w = 8$ ft, $h = 2$ ft

18. $l = 14$ cm, $w = 11$ cm, $h = 19$ cm

SA = _____

SA = _____

19. $l = 3\frac{1}{2}$ in., $w = 2\frac{1}{2}$ in., $h = 4\frac{1}{2}$ in.

20. $l = 6.1$ m, $w = 4.4$ m, $h = 5.5$ m

SA = _____

SA = _____

21. A music company wants to design a cardboard box for mailing
a 2-CD set measuring 14.2 cm by 12.4 cm by 2.5 cm. What
is the least amount of cardboard that can be used for the box? _____

Surface Area of a Cylinder

Find the surface area of each cylinder. Use 3.14 for π.

1. _____

6 ft
32 ft

2. _____

6 in.
12 in.

3. _____

9 m
4 m

4. _____
7 cm

17 cm

5. _____
18 mm

7 mm

6. _____

3 yd
4 yd

7. _____
16 cm

21 cm

8. _____

$2\frac{1}{4}$ in. $6\frac{1}{2}$ in.

9. _____
2.9 cm

2.2 cm

10. _____
10 ft

2 ft

11. _____

13 mm
42 mm

12. _____
15 in.

18 in.

13. _____
1.6 m

1.8 m

14. _____
7 yd

6 yd

15. _____

$3\frac{3}{4}$ in.
8 in.

16. _____
41 cm
98 cm

Given the radius and height of each cylinder, find the surface area.
Use 3.14 for π.

17. $r = 3.8$, $h = 15$

SA ≈ _____

18. $r = 21$, $h = 4$

SA ≈ _____

19. $r = 12$, $h = 13$

SA ≈ _____

20. $r = 2.1$, $h = 4.9$

SA ≈ _____

21. $r = 7.1$, $h = 40$

SA ≈ _____

22. $r = 18$, $h = 11.5$

SA ≈ _____

23. An oatmeal box has the shape of a cylinder with diameter
$3\frac{7}{8}$ in. and height 7 in. What is the surface area of the box? _____

Section 11A Review

Classify each solid. If it is a polyhedron, tell how many vertices, edges, and faces it has.

1. _____
V: __ E: __ F: __

2. _____
V: __ E: __ F: __

3. _____
V: __ E: __ F: __

4. _____
V: __ E: __ F: __

5. _____
V: __ E: __ F: __

6. _____
V: __ E: __ F: __

Find the surface area of each figure.

7. _____

7.3 cm
4.8 cm   9.7 cm
5.5 cm

8. _____

22 in.
21 in.

9. _____

14 ft
11 ft
11 ft

10. _____

5 mm
18 mm

11. Find the surface area of a rectangular prism that measures 15 in. by 21 in. by 24 in.

_____

12. The symbol at the right is used to represent "clubs" in a deck of playing cards. Tell whether the symbol has line symmetry. If it does, draw all the lines of symmetry. [Lesson 8-8]

_____

13. The distance from Berlin, Germany, to Rome, Italy, is about 734 miles. It is also 1181 kilometers. Using these measurements, find the number of kilometers in a mile. [Lesson 10-6]

_____

Three-Dimensional Figures

Draw the front, side, and top views of each solid. There are no hidden cubes.

1.

2.

3.

4.

Describe each pattern. How many cubes are in the eighth solid of each pattern?

5. _____

_____

_____

6. _____

_____

_____

7. Each cube in the solid shown is 5 in. by 5 in. by 5 in.

a. How many cubes are in the solid? _____

b. How tall is the solid at its highest point? _____

c. How wide is the solid at its widest point? _____

Exploring Volume

Find the volume of each solid.

1. _____

2. _____

3. _____

4. _____

5. _____

6. _____

7. _____

8. _____

9. _____

10. _____

11. _____

12. _____

13. A farmer is loading bales of hay onto a wagon. The bales can fit 4 across, and there are 9 rows of bales from the front to the back of the truck. If each stack is to be 5 bales high, how many bales will fit in the wagon?

_____

Calculating Volume

Find the volume of each solid.

1. _____

5 cm
6 cm
17 cm

2. _____

4 in.
5 in.
5 in.

3. _____

2 m
7 m
8 m

4. _____

3 ft
7 ft
5 ft

5. _____

15 cm
5 cm
4 cm

6. _____

8 in.
8 in.
8 in.

7. _____

3 m
16 m
16 m

8. _____

3 yd
3 yd
8 yd

9. _____

3 cm
2 cm
1 cm

10. _____

4 ft
$3\frac{1}{2}$ ft
7 ft

11. _____

15 mm
12 mm
8 mm

12. _____

20 in.
5 in.
5 in.

13. _____

3.2 m
3.2 m
7 m

14. _____

3 ft
1 ft
$2\frac{1}{2}$ ft

15. _____

4 in.
$7\frac{1}{2}$ in.
$3\frac{3}{4}$ in.

16. _____

5.5 cm
7.3 cm
6.2 cm

17. _____

28 mm
12 mm
9 mm

18. _____

11 yd
7 yd
20 yd

19. _____

$3\frac{3}{4}$ in.
6 in.
$2\frac{1}{4}$ in.

20. _____

8.2 cm
5.2 cm
31.4 cm

21. The Panama Canal has a length of 89,200 yd, a width of 37 yd, and a depth of 14 yd. Estimate the volume of water in the canal by assuming it has the shape of a rectangular prism.

Section 11B Review

Find the volume of each solid.

1. _____

2. _____

3. _____

4. _____

5. _____

7 m   6 m   4.5 m

6. _____

8 ft   9 ft   6 ft

7. _____

19.4 cm   6.3 cm   28.5 cm

8. _____

12 in. $4\frac{1}{2}$ in. $6\frac{1}{4}$ in.

Draw the front, side, and top views of each solid. There are no hidden cubes.

9.

10.

11. **Science** Mercury revolves around the sun every 88 days. This is about $\frac{11}{28}$ of the time it takes Venus to revolve around the sun. How long does it take Venus to revolve once around the sun? *[Lesson 7-4]*

_____

12. A rectangle has sides of 10 cm and 15 cm. A similar rectangle has a base that is 24 cm long. There are two possible values for the height of the larger rectangle. What are they? *[Lesson 10-7]*

_____

Cumulative Review Chapters 1–11

Solve. *[Lesson 6-3]*

1. $x + \dfrac{3}{7} = \dfrac{3}{4}$

2. $k - \dfrac{2}{3} = \dfrac{1}{6}$

3. $m + \dfrac{11}{8} = \dfrac{9}{5}$

4. $z - \dfrac{7}{10} = \dfrac{2}{15}$

$x =$ _____

$k =$ _____

$m =$ _____

$z =$ _____

Estimate what percent of each figure is shaded. *[Lesson 10-9]*

5. _____

6. _____

7. _____

8. _____

  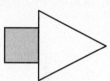

Convert to a percent. *[Lesson 10-10]*

9. 0.16 _____

10. 0.03 _____

11. 0.816 _____

12. 0.56 _____

13. $\dfrac{7}{10}$ _____

14. $\dfrac{3}{25}$ _____

15. $\dfrac{63}{100}$ _____

16. $\dfrac{3}{8}$ _____

17. $\dfrac{17}{20}$ _____

18. $\dfrac{3}{40}$ _____

19. $\dfrac{2}{5}$ _____

20. $\dfrac{3}{4}$ _____

Classify each solid. If it is a polyhedron, tell how many vertices, edges, and faces it has. *[Lesson 11-1]*

21. _____

22. _____

23. _____

V: ___ E: ___ F: ___

V: ___ E: ___ F: ___

V: ___ E: ___ F: ___

Find the volume of each solid. *[Lesson 11-7]*

24. _____

25. _____

26. _____

27. _____

5 ft
13 ft
8 ft

26 m
7 m
7 m

13 in.
$7\frac{1}{2}$ in.
$6\frac{1}{2}$ in.

9.3 cm
11.6 cm
7.8 cm

Name _____

Probability

A set of 12 cards is labeled 1 through 12. Suppose you choose one
card at random. Find the probability of each event.

1. *P*(5) _____   **2.** *P*(even number) _____   **3.** *P*(multiple of 5) _____

4. *P*(12) _____   **5.** *P*(less than 9) _____   **6.** *P*(multiple of 3) _____

A set of 15 tiles is labeled 1 through 15. Suppose you choose one tile
at random. Find the probability of each event.

7. *P*(8) _____   **8.** *P*(7 or 11) _____   **9.** *P*(less than 20) _____

10. *P*(odd number) _____   **11.** *P*(multiple of 3) _____   **12.** *P*(35) _____

Suppose you roll a number cube. Find the probability of each event.

13. *P*(4) _____   **14.** *P*(8) _____   **15.** *P*(2 or 5) _____

16. *P*(less than 4) _____   **17.** *P*(greater than 5) _____   **18.** *P*(multiple of 5) _____

There are 13 cards that spell out L I E C H T E N S T E I N. Suppose
you choose one card. Find the probability of each event.

19. *P*(L) _____   **20.** *P*(I) _____   **21.** *P*(E) _____

22. *P*(N) _____   **23.** *P*(vowel) _____   **24.** *P*(consonant) _____

The bar graph shows the music preference of 28 students
in Gregory's class. If a student is chosen at random, find
the probability of each event.

25. *P*(country) _____   **26.** *P*(rock or rap) _____

27. *P*(classical/jazz) _____   **28.** *P*(country or rock) ___

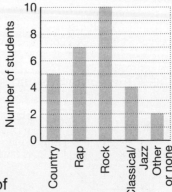

29. Social Science In 1992, there were 100 U.S. Senators, of
whom 43 were Republicans. What is the probability that a
Senator chosen at random from this group would be a
Republican? Express your answer as a decimal and a percent. _____

Making Predictions

Use the data recorded in the chart for Exercises 1–3.

Trial	1	2	3	4	5	6	7	8
Outcome	square	circle	square	triangle	circle	square	square	circle

1. How many different outcomes were there? _____

2. How many times was the outcome a circle? _____

3. What is the probability of the outcome being a square? _____

Use the data recorded in the chart for Exercises 4–6.

Trial	1	2	3	4	5	6	7	8
Outcome	blue	yellow	red	blue	green	red	yellow	blue

Trial	9	10	11	12	13	14	15
Outcome	blue	green	red	blue	blue	green	red

4. How many different outcomes were there? _____

5. How many times was the outcome red? _____

6. What is the probability of the outcome being yellow or green? _____

One day, 40 members who came to an athletic club were asked to complete a survey.

Question	Result
Are you male or female?	28 male, 12 female
Are you under 26 years old?	24 yes, 16 no
Do you use weight machines?	32 yes, 8 no
Do you participate in aerobics classes?	14 yes, 26 no

If the athletic club has 870 members, use the survey results to estimate the number of members who:

7. are male _____

8. are 26 or older _____

9. use weight machines _____

10. take aerobics classes _____

Name _____

Geometric Models of Probability

Suppose you drop a token on each shape in Exercises 1–16. Find the
probability of the token landing on the shaded area.

1. _____

2. _____

3. _____

4. _____

5. _____

6. _____

7. _____

8. _____

9. _____

10. _____

11. _____

12. _____

13. _____

14. _____

15. _____

16. _____

17. **Fine Arts** In 1934, Ben Nicholson used carved white boards to
create a work of art resembling the drawing at the right. Suppose
a speck of dust lands randomly on this work of art.

 a. What is the probability that it lands in one of the
 smaller labeled rectangles?

 _____

 b. The circle has a diameter of about 26 cm. What is the
 probability that the dust speck lands in the circle?

 _____

18. If you throw 500 darts at the hexagonal dart board shown,
how many should you expect to land in the shaded area?

_____

Section 12A Review

A set of 8 tiles is numbered 1 through 8. Suppose you choose one tile at random. Find the probability of each event.

1. $P(5)$ _____

2. P(odd number) _____

3. P(multiple of 3) _____

4. $P(10)$ _____

5. P(3 or 5) _____

6. P(prime number) _____

Use the spinner to find each probability.

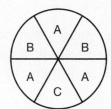

7. $P(A)$ _____

8. $P(B)$ _____

9. $P(C)$ _____

10. P(consonant) _____

11. P(not C) _____

12. P(A or C) _____

13. The probability that a Sloth Airlines flight will be on time is $\frac{2}{15}$. What is the probability that a flight will be late? _____

14. If 160 tokens were dropped on the figure shown, how many would you expect to hit the shaded region?

_____

15. Which probability is greater, 13 out of 35 or 21 out of 57? Explain. _____

16. In Detroit, Michigan, the average probability that it will rain on any given day is about $\frac{9}{25}$. About how many rainy days will there be in a 365-day year? _____

17. If $P(X) = \frac{3}{20}$, $P(Y) = 18\%$, and $P(Z) = 0.2$, which event has the greatest probability of occurring? _____

18. Geography The shaded portion of the figure represents the percent of land used for crops in Ukraine. What percent of Ukraine's land is used for crops? *[Lesson 10-8]*

_____

19. Measurement A carton measuring $5\frac{1}{2}$ in. by 6 in. by 7 in. holds exactly one gallon of liquid. How many cubic inches are in a gallon? *[Lesson 11-6]*

_____

Tree Diagrams

For Exercises 1–4, draw a tree diagram for each situation.

1. A club is choosing a girl (Kathy, Linda, or Meg) and a boy (Warren or Xavier) to represent the club at a student council meeting.

2. You can have a cup or a bowl of soup. The flavors are split pea, minestrone, tomato, and cream of broccoli.

3. A coin is flipped three times in a row.

4. You are going horseback riding. You can choose one of 8 horses, and you may go to any one of 5 destinations. How many different ways can you make your selection? _____

5. If you spin both spinners at the same time, how many possible outcomes are there?

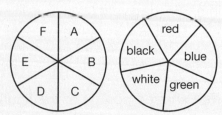

6. Gerald is taking a multiple-choice test in his Spanish class. The test has four questions, and each question has 5 possible answers.

   a. How many different ways can Gerald complete his answer sheet? _____

   b. Gerald forgot to study. If he guesses randomly, what is the probability that he will get the first problem right? _____

Name _____

Compound Events

Five cards numbered 1, 2, 3, 4, and 5 are in a paper bag. Each time a
card is drawn it is replaced. Find the probability of each event.

1. P(even, then even) ___   **2.** P(even, then odd) ____   **3.** P(odd, then even) _____

4. P(odd, then odd) ____   **5.** P(odd, odd, odd) ____   **6.** P(even, even, odd) _____

For Exercises 7–10, the spinner is spun twice.

7. Find the probability of spinning N both times. _____

8. Find the probability of spinning E then R. _____

9. Find the probability of spinning a vowel then a consonant. _____

10. Find the probability of not spinning B either time. _____

11. Suppose you flip a coin and spin the spinner from Exercise 7.
What is the probability that the coin lands heads and you spin M? _____

12. Suppose you roll 5 number cubes while playing Yahtzee®. What
is the probability of getting a number less than 5 on all of the
number cubes? _____

13. A Thai restaurant offers the curry special shown
at the right. If a customer makes all choices
randomly, what is the probability that she orders
a yellow or green tofu curry with tea?

Curry Special $5.99
Curried vegetables with your choice of beef, chicken, tofu, or shrimp.
Choose yellow curry, green curry, or red curry.
Drink included: tea or soda.

_____

14. A standard deck of 52 playing cards includes 26 black cards
(13 clubs and 13 spades) and 26 red cards (13 hearts and
13 diamonds). Suppose you draw a card, put it back, and then
draw again. Find each probability.

    a. P(black, then red) __   **b.** P(red, then spade) ___   **c.** P(heart, then heart) ____

15. The game of Scrabble® includes 100 lettered tiles. 42 of the tiles
represent vowels. If you select a tile, put it back, and select again,
what is the probability of getting a vowel both times? _____

Fairness and Unfairness

For Exercises 1–9, determine if the game is fair. If it is *not*, tell which player has the higher probability of winning.

1. A number cube is tossed. Evan wins if the number is even. Otherwise, Arnold wins.

_____

2. Tina and Jody use a computer to select two random numbers from 1 to 10. Tina wins if both numbers are prime or neither is prime. If one number is prime and the other is not, Jody wins.

_____

3. Kim and Lance played a coin toss game 25 times. Kim won 60% of the games and Lance won 40%.

_____

4. Two number cubes are tossed. If both numbers are even, Amy wins. If both numbers are odd, Brad wins. Otherwise, Cheryl wins.

_____

5. A random number from 1 to 9 is selected. If the number is 5 or greater, Kelly wins. If it is less than 5, Hoang wins.

_____

6. Three coins are tossed. If there are more heads than tails, Beth wins. Otherwise, Dara wins.

_____

7. **Fine Arts** The color pairs on opposite sides of the spinner shown (such as blue and orange) are called *complementary colors.* The spinner is spun twice. If the two colors are the same or complementary, Steve wins. Otherwise, Anson wins.

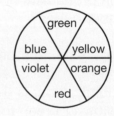

_____

8. The spinner in Exercise 7 is spun twice. If the two colors are the same or next to each other on the spinner, Kyle wins. Otherwise, Francis wins.

_____

9. Carol, James, Nancy, and Tara played a card game 28 times. Tara made a bar graph to show how many times each player won. Can you be certain that the game was fair?

Card Game Winners

_____

Section 12B Review

1. Suppose you roll three different-colored number cubes.

   a. How many outcomes are there? _____

   b. What is the probability for each outcome? _____

2. A fast-food restaurant gives you one of 5 different drinking glasses with each meal. If you order 2 meals, what is the possibility that your drinking glasses will match? _____

3. Eileen is making cupcakes. Each cupcake is made with either chocolate or vanilla cake and chocolate, vanilla, or mint frosting. Each cupcake also has either chopped nuts or colored sprinkles. How many different kinds of cupcakes can Eileen make? _____

4. Your uncle tells you that his license plate has 5 digits, and each digit is either 2, 4, or 6.

   a. How many different license plates can match this description? _____

   b. If you try to guess the license plate, what is the probability that you guess correctly? _____

5. A random 2-digit number (10 to 99) is chosen. Anthony wins if the tens digit is greater than the units digit. Otherwise, Carlos, wins. Is the game fair? Explain.

   _____

   _____

6. Two nickels and a dime are tossed. Candy wins if the value of the coins that come up heads is greater than the value of the coins that come up tails. Otherwise, Frederick wins. Is the game fair? Explain.

   _____

   _____

7. The average daily minimum temperature for January is −14°F in Gulkana, Alaska, and 3°F in Minneapolis, Minnesota. How much warmer is the temperature in Minneapolis than in Gulkana? *[Lesson 9-3]* _____

8. A can of fancy mixed nuts has diameter 10.0 cm and height 9.3 cm. Find the surface area of the can. *[Lesson 11-4]* _____

Cumulative Review Chapters 1–12

What is the least rotation that will land the figure on top of itself? *[Lesson 8-9]*

1. _____

2. _____

3. _____

4. _____

Solve each proportion. *[Lesson 10-5]*

5. $\dfrac{15}{10} = \dfrac{6}{t}$

$t =$ _____

6. $\dfrac{3}{h} = \dfrac{9}{15}$

$h =$ _____

7. $\dfrac{10}{f} = \dfrac{6}{27}$

$f =$ _____

8. $\dfrac{q}{10} = \dfrac{12}{8}$

$q =$ _____

9. $\dfrac{40}{4} = \dfrac{m}{5}$

$m =$ _____

10. $\dfrac{w}{8} = \dfrac{4}{16}$

$w =$ _____

11. $\dfrac{15}{18} = \dfrac{v}{24}$

$v =$ _____

12. $\dfrac{15}{u} = \dfrac{12}{40}$

$u =$ _____

Find the surface area. *[Lesson 11-3]*

13. _____

6.9 m
8.0 m
2.8 m

14. _____
21 ft
21 ft
21 ft

15. _____

18 cm
13 cm
13 cm

16. _____

$2\frac{1}{2}$ in.
9 in.
7 in.

There are 12 cards that spell out C O N S T I T U T I O N. Suppose you choose one card. Find the probability of each event. *[Lesson 12-1]*

17. $P(\text{C})$ _____

18. $P(\text{O})$ _____

19. $P(\text{T})$ _____

20. $P(\text{vowel})$ _____

21. $P(\text{N or O})$ _____

22. $P(\text{consonant})$ _____

23. $P(\text{Z})$ _____

24. $P(\text{T or I})$ _____

25. $P(\text{not a T})$ _____

Suppose you drop a token on each shape. Find the probability of the token landing on the shaded area. *[Lesson 12-3]*

26. _____

8 in.

27. _____

28. _____

29. _____